COMPELLING CHORAL CONCERTS
13 CREATIVE PROGRAMS WITH NARRATION

Advance Praise for *Compelling Choral Concerts*

Linda Powell has a knack for pulling together varied and interesting repertoire and completing it with interesting bits of history and background information. Her programs always come together so beautifully because of her passion, vision, and attention to detail. Additionally she shares the behind-the-scenes technical work that is needed for a smashing program. This will save every choral director loads of time!

> Marta Johnson
> *Musician*

Her programs reflect an extraordinary attention to detail as well as real showmanship. Any music teacher who wants a program to grow should read Linda's book.

> Dr. Antonia Bouillette
> *Principal*
> *Trinity High School,*
> *River Forest, Illinois*

Our choral concerts were more than just that—they were performances. Each program had a central theme, and with all of the elements, the carefully chosen songs, the planned and playful (and often theatrical) entrances, the well-written narrations and the choreography, we told a story.

> Ola Wysocki
> *Trinity High School student*

COMPELLING CHORAL CONCERTS

13 CREATIVE PROGRAMS WITH NARRATION

LINDA CRABTREE POWELL

WITH NARRATIONS BY
VALERIE SOKOL AND JULIA BUCKLEY

GIA Publications, Inc.
Chicago

> Dedicated to a dear friend, colleague, director, and mentor
> Valerie Sokol (1942–2013)
> Narrator, *Compelling Choral Concerts*

GIA Publications, Inc.
7404 South Mason Avenue
Chicago, IL 60638
www.giamusic.com
G-8810
© 2014 GIA Publications, Inc.

All rights reserved.
Printed in the United States of America
ISBN: 978-1-62277-110-3

Table of Contents

Foreword		vii
Introduction		ix
Themed Choral Planning		1

SPRING PROGRAMS

And Nature Sings	*Valerie Sokol*	16
Back to Beatles	*Valerie Sokol*	22
The Birds and the Bees	*Valerie Sokol*	32
Moments from Musicals	*Valerie Sokol*	44
Musical Conversations	*Valerie Sokol*	56
The Spirit Says SING!	*Valerie Sokol and Linda Crabtree Powell*	68

WINTER PROGRAMS

Angels	*Valerie Sokol*	78
Be Joyful!	*Julia Buckley and Linda Crabtree Powell*	88
Colors of Christmas	*Valerie Sokol and Linda Crabtree Powell*	98
Food, Fun, and Festivities!	*Julia Buckley and Linda Crabtree Powell*	110
A Light in Night	*Valerie Sokol and Linda Crabtree Powell*	118
Miracles	*Valerie Sokol, Barbara D'Asaro, and Linda Crabtree Powell*	126
'Tis the Season	*Valerie Sokol and Linda Crabtree Powell*	136

Choral Repertoire Inventory	147
About the Authors	157

Foreword

I have known Linda Crabtree Powell for over a decade. During that time, I have admired her thoughtful and innovative approach to creating concert programs. When I attend Linda's choral concerts, I am always delighted with the combinations of musical, visual, and spoken aspects of her performances.

I believe that all choral directors want to create a magical experience on stage for our singers and audiences. How to achieve that experience is the challenge that Linda is addressing here. Sometimes, an artfully strung sequence of choral octavos is sufficient. At other times, the addition of narration and/or staging can allow the musical program to truly blossom with greatly increased emotional impact. This is where Linda's work has such value for the field.

This book contains combinations of musical selections, spoken readings, and staging that Linda has developed over many years. These are actual concerts that have been presented and really work. You can use these materials in several ways. Perhaps, at first, you may want to use one of her programs just "as is," and I expect that you'll have a great time doing just that. However, I sincerely hope that, over the years of trying out concerts in this way, you will become more confident to use these "conversations" as jumping-off points for *your own* creativity. I hope that you will enjoy weaving in your own favorite readings and staging ideas, perhaps working with students or colleagues to create your own fabrics of concert presentations. In my own creative life, this work has taken on more and more importance over the years. Perhaps you too will develop a similar love for this sort of programming. It is a richly rewarding approach to engaging not only your own creativity but that of your whole community.

What you hold in your hands is a tremendous resource. Linda's examples here will guide you to create inspiring choral concerts in the years to come. I encourage you to use this book fully, to challenge and engage your singers, to entertain and touch the hearts of your audiences, and to energize your ongoing work as a choral director.

—Jonathan Miller
Founder and Artistic Director
Chicago *a cappella*
Chorus America board member,
2009–2014

Introduction

This collection of themed programs with narration was written over a period of several years with the intent of creating concerts that were more cohesive. Their form and style of presentation gradually developed from the idea of using choral pieces linked by a central theme or topic, with a narration or dialogue related to the theme and the music. Unlike instrumental music, choral music has the advantage of lyrics that help convey a message. These programs connect choral pieces with an original spoken script between the pieces, creating a conversation between the words and the music.

Initially, the themed choral project began with the intention of covering transitions in the concert when choirs were entering or leaving the stage, and to redirect the audience's attention between the musical selections. Previous programs seemed to lose their flow or sense of timing with the interruption of groups moving into place or off the stage. The smooth transitions through the program, achieved by using the narration and music together, gave an overall form to the concert and added needed continuity to the performance.

The second reason that these programs were created was that choral programs sometimes were disjointed, even with well-planned repertoire, and it could be hard for audiences to remember what music they heard. Also, there needed to be an easy way for the students and audience to refer to the concert, and that happened with a title that identified the theme. The title, with the music and the narration, made the program clear and complete.

With the collaboration of another writer, I started considering incorporating a narration that ran through the concert, not just an introduction, with a complementary script based on the lyrics in the program. The lyrics from the music and the words in the script were related. When this type of combination happened with the script and the music, the audience became engaged in looking at and listening to the choir and the narrator(s). Together, the themed choral concept connected the program in a natural, interesting way.

I created these programs for the students at Trinity High School, which is a Sinsinawa Dominican college preparatory school for young women. There were only a few girls participating in the choir when I started, so I wanted to find a way to involve more students, and also to find a way to add boys to join in singing music from the SATB repertoire, too. There are differences in levels of difficulty in the repertoire in each of these programs, from beginning through advanced choirs, as well as a variety of voicing (treble voices, mixed voices, unison, and so on). Every school has different combinations of types of choirs and amounts of scheduled rehearsal time, so the programs here include pieces that are available in a variety of vocal combinations.

The programs in this book will save directors an immense amount of time because the planning and writing have already been done. You only need to choose which voicing of each piece you will need to buy; the inventory of the music used in these programs (see page 147) includes information about the available versions. (Since music goes out of print, check with your music retailer about the arrangements for various voicings—SATB, SSA, or others—that are still available for purchase.)

Ideally, you will be able to perform these programs exactly as they are written, because they have been created as an entirety. However, depending on your circumstances, you may want or need to add or substitute a different piece of music related to the theme. Not every piece of music has to have a narration before it, but the placement of the piece in the order of the program is very important. Consider the new addition as it relates to the music that precedes and follows it in terms of style, tempo, key or mode (major or minor), instrumentation, vocal difficulty, and text. Ideas about where and how to find and choose additional or substitute pieces for these programs are in the next chapter.

Each program in this collection is distinctly different. Seven are specifically for winter, and six are for spring (some might work at any time of the year). Most of the programs offered here for winter are related to Christmas in some way, but include both sacred and secular music. There are two options for the narration before each piece that has a sacred text, so you can pick one that fits your situation best. (Some schools allow both sacred and secular choral music, but some only approve secular music, so you might want to make some substitutions to the repertoire.) The *Food, Fun, and Festivities!* winter program is entirely secular.

Compelling Choral Concerts include musical balance and variety for winter and spring programs. This collection of programs is intended to inspire and assist choral directors and present new possibilities for using themes with an accompanying narration in performance.

My thanks and acknowledgements are extended to GIA Publications, Alec Harris, Kirin Nielsen, Valerie Sokol, Julia Buckley, Jonathan Miller, William Lea, Barbara D'Asaro, Diana Robin, Ron Orzel, Martha Albers, Marta Johnson, Valerie DePriest, Don Sokol, Tina Reynolds, Trinity High School College Preparatory School for Women, Dan Vogt, Michelle

INTRODUCTION

Germanson, OP, Dr. Antonia C. Bouillette, Kelly Banos, Viki Siliunas, Patti Williams, Samantha Gay, Theoni Richardson, Dana Dahhan, Ola Wysocki, Jonah Figueroa, Emily Mott, Daphne Nelson, Katie Sreenan, and Gordon Powell, who all helped in making these programs and project possible.

—Linda Crabtree Powell

Planning a Themed Choral Program

You can learn to create thematic programs with narration, too. It takes a lot of planning but is fun to do! Programs of this kind have the components of a musical theater production, but the emphasis is always on the choral repertoire. By adding a narrative or storyline that ties together the musical compositions, and that is based on the lyrics in the pieces, the program becomes a dramatic concert.

Selecting the Music

The most important component of your program is the music: Select it carefully, and select it first. A choral director should always be listening to and gathering music possibilities, including sample copies for your file. Developing your own choral library of individual pieces is a continual process. Think of your programming as something similar to how an opera season is planned several years in advance: You want to have selections available that you have been considering and saving for that specific program, and that means adding to and trimming your score collection continuously.

Try keeping your collection of octavos in theme categories. In a typical music publisher's catalog, the music will be divided into sections such as Christmas, sacred, spirituals, pop, musicals, and other categories. Instead of organizing my library that way, I try grouping the pieces by larger themes, such as nature, literature in lyrics, weather, animals, folk songs, transportation, love, seasons, or whatever strikes me as a possible area for the development of a program idea. Look at both the music and the lyrics to decide how to group the musical works. I look for what I consider to be a group of strong pieces of repertoire and then I will tie them together with a common theme.

The repertoire used in the concert programs in this book includes some rediscovered arrangements of classic melodies that are many years old but are still interesting. It was fun to find them among old files. If it is necessary to substitute or augment your program, always look to see what you have—sometimes it will surprise you.

Unfortunately, music can go out of print quickly. (Using photocopies instead of buying original copies is a major cause of this.) Even during the course of writing these programs, some of the music became unavailable. It is still included for your reference; maybe you have these pieces tucked away, too. Otherwise, these selections are probably not going to be easily available.

Therefore, there is another recommended arrangement in the repertoire list for each program.

While it is eventually preferable to establish your own choral library, the internet is an excellent resource for previewing and selecting choral music and for seeing new publications. Some of the major sites to explore are Choralnet.org, Musica.net, and CPDL (Choral Public Domain Library: www2.cpdl.org/wiki/index.php/Main_Page). Choralnet resources include lists of pieces organized by concert topic, and Musica.net is an international database of choral music that is searchable by topic, keyword, or other criteria. CPDL is a searchable library of choral scores that can be printed and used for free.

Other professional organizations include repertoire lists on their websites and are valuable as information resources, including American Choral Directors Association (ACDA; www.acda.org), National Association for Music Education (NAfME; www.nafme.org), and Chorus America (chorusamerica.org). Look at their music selections for state festivals. That is music that has already been chosen by choral teachers. Checking the festivals and other music programs can be very helpful in making selections and getting ideas. Working with your colleagues—schools, churches, or performing ensembles—and borrowing music is also a good possibility. Some publishers will send you perusal copies, and some have subscriptions for sample copies. Peeking at what you can see and hear online is great, but it isn't a completely satisfactory alternative to seeing the complete score. Whenever possible, attend choral reading sessions that are offered in your area by publishing companies or at choral conferences. Many composers now self-publish, too, so hearing something unique may be available only through that individual.

Developing the Concert Theme

Now it's time to develop your concert theme. How does that work? Well perhaps you begin noticing you like music about nature, so start keeping it together or gathering the titles that might be related. When you realize you have a common thread in the titles or lyrics, you can start adding other pieces. Let's look at *The Birds and the Bees* on page 32. This program began with the idea of songs about nature, but then evolved into music about spring, with birds, with bees, then even love!

After you have collected music related to your intended theme, start examining the repertoire more closely. You are assembling a program of music related in theme but contrasting in styles. Start with more pieces than you think you can use for a program and then edit as you go along. See how the pieces compare with one another.

You are considering many elements for the program order. The lyrics need to have something in common with each other, yet there needs to be musical diversity. Imagine how each selection works in the context of the entire program. Look at different arrangements when you have chosen the tunes you have decided to use. Consider the key, vocal ranges, accompaniment or not, instrumentation, tempo, style, level of difficulty, duration, musical form, and the educational value.

These considerations have already been made for you in the programs included in this book. Each program contains specific and carefully examined arrangements. What you select for a program should be music you love and that the choir will learn and love.

An important factor for programs is the order in which the choirs will be singing. Select the music and the voicing to match the choirs' levels and as it relates to the complete program shape. All the voicing options are listed in the choral repertoire inventory. Usually the more difficult repertoire in a program is near the end so usually that is where your more advanced choir would be placed. Consider music that will challenge each performing group. For contrast, learn a good novelty or lighter number that can be an audience favorite and will have taken a much smaller amount of rehearsal time; think about including humor and what each group will be preparing in total. The singers need to be challenged and they need to have fun singing.

Create a title for the program. This has been an idea you have been considering as you have assembled your music. The title might change as you focus your theme, but it can be useful to keep in mind while you decide on the final program repertoire. Look at your music titles and lyrics to come up with ideas. The program title should be something short and easy to remember. You will be using those words to publicize your performance and to help you add other aspects to your program such as stage decorations, color schemes, stage attire, and more.

Structuring the Program

The choral program basically contains an opening, middle, and closing. Plan a strong musical opening, a body including the program content of selected repertoire, and an effective closing. Try not to get stuck in a certain predictable mold. Consider what can be performed as an encore.

The Concert Opening

The first piece of music will set the tone for your concert. The audience will form an immediate impression with the opening, so it should be very well prepared and something you have thought about for the first sounds they will hear from your choir. There are many ways to begin programs, and using varying ways at your concerts is a good idea. You might start with a high-energy piece for combined choirs, a processional, a soloist, or something else.

Here are some types of concert openings with examples from the programs in this collection:

Type	Title	Program
processional	Down to the River to Pray	*And Nature Sings*
surrounding the audience	It's the Most Wonderful Time of the Year	*Be Joyful!*
unison	The Birds and the Bees	*The Birds and the Bees*
soloist	Tonight	*Moments from Musicals*
uplifting	If Music Be the Food of Love How Can I Keep from Singing	*Musical Conversations* *The Spirit Says SING!*
creative	Prayer from *Hansel and Gretel* (with candles) Angels We Have Heard on High (with handchimes) She Loves You! (movie clip)	*Angels* *Miracles* *Back to the Beatles*
beginning message	Christmas Time Is Here Jesu, Joy of Man's Desiring	*Colors of Christmas* *A Light in the Night*
high energy	It's the Most Wonderful Time of the Year Jingle Bells	*Be Joyful!* *Food, Fun, and Festivities!*

The Program Body

The body of the program should be designed with all musical decisions made *before* considering the narration or script. Variety should be considered in the total form of the program. Imagine how one piece of music sounds when it ends and how the next one will follow. While you are trying to avoid similar tempi and similar styles in a sequence of pieces, some contrasts can be too abrupt. Consider how the lyrics follow each other from piece to piece. Other factors to consider are the placement of a cappella selections, when you have soloists, the size of the ensembles/choirs, other instrumentation being used, and the general flow of the music. Also consider the logistics of moving props on or off stage, varied visual formations, and the order of performance by the different choirs (limiting the number of entrances and exits). If possible, include solo pieces in the concert; these contrast well with choral pieces, and audiences like to hear individual voices. Lay out your program order and see how it looks and how you think it will sound. All of the programs included in this book are approximately one hour long. They are written intentionally without an intermission. The narration will segue from one musical selection to the next and keep the program continuity moving along.

The Finale

The closing of the program is the final sound you want to be remembered. There are many ways to have effective closes.

The closing is *almost* the end of the program. The audience's applause shows their appreciation for the total concert. It will be well deserved, so don't rush off.

Prepare your choirs and technical help for what you want to have happen after the last piece. Will the students take a collective bow? Will the choir(s) sing an encore? What is the best way for the choir(s) to exit? Will the curtain close immediately? After all of your previous preparation, plan the final moments so they are not disorganized. There should be a specific final cue from the director for the choirs and the technical help.

Let the audience be surprised the program is over so quickly; they should be eager to return for your next concert. Plan a reception following the concert so there is an opportunity for the audience and the performers to mingle and enjoy themselves together.

Here are some closing ideas, with examples from the programs:

Type	Title	Program
reflective	Dona Nobis Pacem	*And Nature Sings*
audience sing	All You Need is Love	*Back to the Beatles*
audience	a familiar Christmas carol	*'Tis the Season*
tradition	alumni joining the choir in the last piece	winter programs
reprise	The Birds and the Bees	*The Birds and the Bees*
creative	choral reading ("Master of Music" poem)	*Musical Conversations*
composition premiere	Litany to St. Cecilia	*Miracles*
spiritual	I'm Gonna Sing When the Spirit Says Sing	*The Spirit Says SING!*
	Jordan's Angels	*Angels*
	Angels Watchin' Over Me	*A Light in the Night*
big ending	You Can't Stop the Beat	*Moments from Musicals*
	Sleigh Ride	*Food, Fun, and Festivities!*
combined choirs	Sing for Joy!	*Be Joyful!*

Links to YouTube videos of excerpts from performances of some of the programs are available at www.giamusic.com/ccc.

Narration and Narrators

You have decided on the music and the program title—now for the narration. This element will inform the audience about the musical theme while giving the singers the time to get in place and be ready to perform. This continuity is what gives the program a sense of flow and professionalism. You are using the script or narration to connect the musical selections and redirect the audience's attention visually and aurally.

The narrations in the programs presented here were all written in collaboration with a professional colleague. This involved working together by talking about the music to come up with ideas and a story line. The narration can be basic—sharing background information about the music—or it may develop into a completely independent dialogue around the pieces.

You may be fortunate to have other musicians where you work or teach, but frequently you may be the only musician around. That doesn't mean you can't get help. A themed choral program can be a somewhat complex production with more than one component. Find colleagues who are interested in the arts and who might have expertise to contribute; use the talents that are around you.

For example, the language arts teacher would be an excellent choice to help you with writing a complementary script. The visual arts teacher may be willing to have art students help with your publicity. (The publicity poster could be an excellent project for an art class.) Perhaps your physical education department would like to incorporate some dance elements.

The narrators present the spoken words that link your music with the theme, and they have an important role in communicating with the audience. I recommended that the narrators not be members of the choir because of the stage movement that happens during the narration, and so the audience can focus on either the narrator or choir without distractions or interruptions. It is difficult for a student to be involved in both narrating and singing.

The narrators should receive vocal coaching from a teacher or director. They should have their scripts at least one month prior to the concert in order to become familiar with their individual lines and the complete program dialogue. Each narrator should have a prepared script in a three-ring binder; his or her individual lines should be highlighted in yellow and the unison lines should be highlighted in pink. Just like the choir, the narrators should receive specific stage directions and should mark their lines with instructions for saying them. Listen to the narrators and identify the words that should be emphasized as they relate to the music. The tempo of the speaking voices should be varied, and the narrators should use clear diction with exaggerated consonants. Their faces and voices should be expressive, and they should have confident posture while entering, performing, and exiting. If there is a speech program offered by the school, there may be students who are already experienced with speaking in public and are comfortable on stage. It is important that the narrators rehearse with each other as well as together with the choir. If possible, they should memorize sections of the narration so they are able to use their eyes and faces to communicate with the audience. Narrators should be positioned in varying locations during the program, depending on choir entrances and exits.

Staging Ideas

Variety adds interest to your programs. Sometimes the audience will remember the little things best. There are always vast differences in your students' talents and experience, so think about them when preparing your program.

If you have strong individual voices, consider having a soloist sing sections of a piece or including a solo song. If you have strong instrumentalists, find places in the music when they can accompany your choir. If you have strong dancers, add dancing. Consider using a small prop for a piece of music in all of your programs, such as umbrellas, beads, egg shakers, kazoos, fans, or flashlights. Choreography should include the total choir at some point; a little movement can go a long way in a performance—and even a choir director can come up with some great moves! But don't forget: The best part of a choral concert is hearing the choir!

Staging ideas to add to your performances are included before each of the programs in this book. You may also be inspired to create some of your own.

Performance Preparation

Some of the following recommendations are what you will want to use with any choral program, and some are particular to achieving the format of a continual production on the stage for the themed program. These suggestions will help you organize the details beyond the music and the narration, and include additional considerations involved in a performance.

Promotion and Publicity

Your choir deserves an appreciative audience. As a music educator, it is your responsibility and to your benefit to promote all of the arts through the choral program. Use as many different kinds of media as you can to publicize what you are doing. Posting beautiful posters in the school, community, churches, and businesses is a good start. The posters we used for our performances of these programs are included before each concert script as inspiration for your own artwork. (Please do not duplicate or imitate these pieces of art, which are the property of the artists.) Use web pages and social media such as Facebook, Twitter, Tumblr, and more to advertise your concert. Usually a school has an employee or department that can assist you with these, particularly if you have prepared the information for them.

Choral members can also have wonderful new ideas, so be open to their suggestions and ideas. Students love to wear T-shirts; how about having some made with your program's name on it? This is particularly good if the performers can wear them on the day of the concert. You are trying to create an air of excitement for that event, so use announcements, school and community newspaper articles, and these other methods to build anticipation.

After the performance, publicity is just as important as before. Perhaps you have had someone film the entire concert, and now there is the great opportunity to share the performance on YouTube or in other venues. If some people missed this performance, you don't want them to miss the next one. Everyone should be eagerly awaiting the next season's programs.

Technology and Lighting

Technology is sometimes the unwanted but necessary part of the performance. Microphones and amplification are essential in most performance spaces. If an audience cannot hear what you are singing and saying, they will not listen for long. In a choral production with narration you will likely have different kinds of needs for microphones: narrators, soloists, and choirs of potentially different sizes. Spend rehearsal time with the mikes and allow enough time to make adjustments. Students should learn how to sing with a mike so that it is familiar to them and a natural part of their performance. Ideally, you should have a professional technician assisting you, but if that's not possible, students are always anxious to be trained in this area.

Lighting obviously lets you see the performance. Keep the house lights up until you are ready to start. Next, stop the preconcert music (music related to the performance), dim the lights, and be ready to go. These steps are setting the tone for your performance. The concert plans in this book also give specific directions for this.

Regardless of what lighting you have available, try to direct the lights to wherever you want your audience to look. This is important because you are keeping the action flowing. The lights can dim on the choir and focus on your narrators while there is activity with entering or exiting the stage—both narration and movement happen at the same time. Typically, an audience watches the choirs gradually come on and go off; this is not what you want. The audience's attention should be directed to the narrator or to the performers who will be in the lights and ready to sing!

If you are using risers, there is a tendency for it to be difficult to see student's faces on the top rows. Some refocusing of the lights is usually required so everyone can be seen clearly.

Stage Sets or Decorations

A little color or a few stage props on your stage can make a big visual impact. Here is where the theme can help you develop a "look" on your stage. Whenever it is possible, use the area over singer's heads. This creates a visual "frame" and looks good in photos, too. Live flowers can also "frame" your stage along the floor, and selling them can be a good fundraising project at the same time. Poinsettias are a good choice for winter programs and geraniums can look nice in spring. Check with your local florist—they are usually willing to help in some way. Don't forget to acknowledge donors and donations in your program.

We have successfully used stage sets and decorations that have included hanging large paper snowflakes and using different sizes of holiday ornaments, flowing colored ribbons, falling "snow," or putting large musical symbols on the walls. Exaggerate the dimensions of what you are using when possible. Again, use your theme in developing what the audience will see on the stage.

Printed Program

You should have a printed program for the audience. This can be simple or elaborate, but it should include every name of all participating students. Check and recheck names and be sure they are spelled correctly. Everyone knows the first thing you do when you look at a program is find your own name. Make sure all of the names are there!

The music selections should be listed in performance order and include the title, composer, lyricist, and arranger. Thanks and acknowledgments should be in the program, so keep track of people or businesses whom you want to include. Perhaps you would want to consider writing a director's statement about the choirs and coming performances.

Final Details

Opening the Program

There may be variations, but the basic guideline for the opening of a performance should be to include prepared recorded music as the audience enters. Consider what music you select so that it has some association with the pieces in the concert. If you have instrumental musicians available, they can play in an area outside of the auditorium or performance area, preceding the concert or immediately after. It is likely there will be already be instrumental musicians needed in some selections of the choral concert.

At the time the performance is scheduled to begin, the house lights should blink and dim to half. There should be an announcement that cell phones and other sound-producing objects should be muted or turned off, and that out of respect for the performers, there should be no flash photography or texting. If a video of the performance will be available, include the information in the house announcement and program. Audience etiquette information can also be printed in the program.

If you are using a traditional stage, close the curtain and project a "curtain warmer," which means focusing lights on the curtain so that the audience has something to look at before the show starts. After the house announcements are finished, the house lights can be lowered the rest of the way and the main curtain can be opened. Bring up the stage lights as this occurs. If there is not a curtain, the lighting cue will substitute as the start of the program. The choir and narrators should already be in place in their predetermined location. Again, narrators are only to speak when they have a light on them. The spotlight, if used, is always turned off when the narrators are finished speaking and before they exit, so the technical crew will also need to have a copy of the narration to follow along.

During the transitions, the choir can either remain standing or use the opportunity to quietly move to a different stage location or into a different standing position.

Stage Attire

Students should have a clearly written explanation of the required concert attire. Black attire offers the most possibilities for variation. You can add colored pieces or costume additions such as scarves, blazers, vests, jackets, beads, and so on. Be specific about defining the length of skirts or dresses. It can also be suitable for the women to wear pants for some performances. Choirs can sometimes purchase exactly the same clothing; however, this can be an expensive option. Students may also have some good suggestions for clothing and accessories. Think of ideas for accessories that may be related to your music titles. Shoes, hair, and accessory guidelines should be included in the directions. Black shoes should not include tennis shoes, boots, or any open toe style. If heels are to be worn by the ladies, they should practice wearing them during a full rehearsal. There should not be any bracelets or necklaces unless they are uniform throughout the group. Normal earrings are fine. The best look for hair on stage is to keep it as simple as possible and to have it pulled off of the face. Be sure to avoid hanging strands that cover the eyes or which need to be constantly pushed back behind an ear. The audience wants to see faces and concentrate on hearing the singing. They do not want to be distracted by nervous hair gestures.

Staging Positions

In a themed program, the singers' position should be assigned with the same directions as would be done for a blocked theater position. This means each singer needs to be given a specific location on the risers or stage so the choir looks and sounds its best, and choir members need to know that position is important. The choral director is responsible for the vocal balance as it relates to the choir placement, and also to the visual picture on the stage. The system of using "windows" with choral singers (your head is centered between the two people you are standing behind) is recommended when on risers or standing in rows. If the singer cannot see the conductor, the singer is not standing in the correct space. Emphasize the importance of the singer's exact assigned location. It is not an arbitrary position. The director is always looking at the total stage picture and needs to be able to see and hear each person.

Consider different choral formations which provide a variety of views for your audience and also change the blend of the sound. There are many possibilities; here are some ideas that may be effective, depending on the piece of music:

- singing in sections
- singing with vocal parts mixed
- spreading out in groups or ensembles (such as SATB quartets)
- performing in areas around the audience
- surrounding the audience in a circle formation
- singing in groups of different sizes, such as alternating the full choir on one verse with a small group on another verse
- using the front and back of the performance area
- varying distances between the singers
- altering heights on the risers or varying the number of rows

The narration allows you that extra time between repertoire to regroup or rearrange. The choral director has time to think instead of turning around and addressing the audience. The choir is setting up, mentally and physically, for their next selection.

A choir's entrance or exit is a continuation of their performance and demonstrates their stage awareness. This needs adequate rehearsal with a basic understanding of stage directions by the choir (stage left: the performers' left side; stage right: the performers' right side; downstage: toward the audience; upstage: away from the audience) as well as awareness of the choral "windows" explained above. While a choir's movement should not be a focus (because the audience is listening to the narration), they should be moving quickly in an energized, confident, and quiet manner. This is important. Many directors under-rehearse the entrances, row order, bows, or exits; however, it is part of what the audience sees and therefore is part of the program. Entrances and exits should be well planned and rehearsed. Know when to come on and when to leave the stage, and allow for applause, too. A good technique for taking a bow is to have the choir members say quietly to themselves during applause "Did I shine my shoes today?" (looking down at them with their heads bowed), then "Yes, I shined my shoes today" (standing straight). It works, and makes the singers smile, too.

Singing and Acting

Having all music memorized for programs is highly recommended! It is important to have a conductor, but there may be some repertoire that can be very effective without you directing and will develop their independent singing and performing abilities. You can also consider using a student conductor.

When the conductor is directing the choir, there has to be total eye contact between the singers and their conductor. The singers and conductor should be using good posture and not fidgeting or displaying any other distracting motions. This takes focus and energy from every singer. When this happens correctly, the music has the effect of communicating, and that makes the performance successful for everyone! The highest compliment from the audience is hearing that split second of silence after the final cutoff after singing a well-prepared piece of music. The choir has communicated the music and the lyrics to the audience. That is the musical level you want to develop with your choir's performance and the appreciation you want to achieve from your audience.

In the programs that are presented here, there are selections for the choirs to sing without needing a conductor, particularly when there is choreography involved. Then the singers get a chance to perform and sing directly to their audience. It takes added rehearsal, but when they are well prepared they will be confident and will like performing on their own. The choir members should use lots of appropriate facial expression while singing and lots of energy in performing, whatever they are singing about! Everybody should be using their eyes to communicate the lyrics and the emotions in the music.

Some examples of repertoire that have worked well without a conductor are: "Forget About the Boy," "You Can't Stop the Beat," "The Birds and the Bees," "Hole in the Bucket," "Won't You Join the Dance," "Monotone Angel," and "Santa Baby." You will be able to find some others, too.

Coda

A themed program with narration is a creative way of presenting your choral repertoire. After you have performed some of these prepared programs, planning yours will be easier to do. Prepare music that is solid repertoire, interesting and fun for your students, for your audience, and for you, too. Enjoy *your* compelling choral concerts!

SPRING PROGRAMS

Trinity High School Fine Arts Department presents

"And Nature Sings"

Spring Fine Arts Evening

*Featuring Bel Coro, Chamber Choir,
Le Ragazze, the Trinity String Ensemble,
and our student artists' recent work.*

Tuesday, May 13th
6~8 pm

TRINITY HIGH SCHOOL AUDITORIUM

Poster by Chloe Dzielak

And Nature Sings

Title	Composer/Lyricist
Down to the River to Pray *O Brother, Where Art Thou?*	Traditional Appalachian hymn arr. Sheldon Curry
For the Beauty of the Earth	John Rutter/Folliot S. Pierpoint
Dust in the Wind	Kerry Livgren arr. Roger Emerson
Stormy Weather	Harold Arlen/Ted Koehler
Over the Rainbow *The Wizard of Oz*	Harold Arlen/Edgar "Yip" Harburg arr. Russell Robinson
Shenandoah	American folk song arr. Ed Lojeski
The Wind	Ruth Elaine Schram
At the River	Robert Lowry adapt. Aaron Copland arr. Raymond Wilding-White
Fly Me to the Moon	Bert Howard arr. Kirby Shaw
Bridge over Troubled Water	Paul Simon arr. Kirby Shaw
Dona nobis pacem (*Give us peace*)	16th century anonymous arr. Hal H. Hopson

In this program the pieces I like to add movement to are the opening "Down to the River to Pray," "Fly Me to the Moon," and "Bridge over Troubled Water." Add a clap-step movement to "Bridge over Troubled Water." You can't sing this standing still!

And Nature Sings

> *Note: The following program is scripted for two narrators, which is the preferred way to presenting the material, but if necessary, it can easily be converted using just one narrator. If two narrators are used, their two voices should blend well, as they will be doing some unison speaking.*

SECTION 1

A: The winter was long, the snow constant and deep.

B: The skies were dark and heavy with cloud

A: and the wind was cold.

B: My heart cried out for spring,

A: for the earth to soften and bloom

B: and so I went to the river, seeking renewal

A & B: and fell on my knees to pray.

Down to the River to Pray

SECTION 2

A: There I found my soul refreshed,

B: for the river was vibrant with rushing water,

A: breaking through the ice and dashing against the old snow.

B: I saw the snowdrop and the crocus shyly nodding their heads.

A & B: It's spring! they said, in colors of white

A: and purple

B: and gold.

A & B: It's spring!

For the Beauty of the Earth

SECTION 3

B: And I realized the heaviness in my heart has gone.

A & B: It has vanished,

B: like the dust in the wind.

Dust in the Wind

SECTION 4

A: Yes, winter has gone, but somehow I remember it well—

A & B: the rain, the snow, the sleet, the cold.

A: I just couldn't seem to get myself together

B: and my life was bare and gloomy.

A & B: There was misery everywhere,

B: there was *(pause)* stormy weather.

Stormy Weather

SECTION 5

B: But here today

A: I see the evidence of spring all around me.

A & B: The storm has gone

A: and the blue sky wears a rainbow as its crown.

Over the Rainbow

SECTION 6

A: I remember another river from long ago

B: a river I played by as a child.

A: Different from this river,

B: the river of my youth was wide and slow as it moved to the sea.

A: I long to return to that time, to my carefree childhood days,

B: and see once again that rolling river,

A & B: my river, the Shenandoah.

Shenandoah

SECTION 7

B: The wind fans my cheek

A: and teases my hair.

B: It calls my name softly as it blows

A: and I answer,

A & B: "I am here."

The Wind

SECTION 8

A: As I stand by the river,

B: the beautiful, beautiful river,

A: I call my friends to me

A & B: and we gather together to sing

A: our praises to the Lord.

At the River

SECTION 9

B: My heart is filled with the joy of spring.

A: It leaps with love!

B: I feel so happy that I could fly!

Fly Me to the Moon

SECTION 10

A: I realize now that when I am troubled,

B: when my heart is heavy

A: and grief threatens to overwhelm me,

B: I can go to nature and find peace

A: in the splendor of the mountains,

B: the delicate blush of a rose,

A: the murmur of the waves kissing the shore.

B: For me, the beauty of the world around me will always be a bridge over troubled water.

Bridge over Troubled Water

SECTION 11

A: If we look at nature and really see it,

B: if we listen and really hear,

A: and if we respect what we see and hear

B: despite our differences,

A: we can live together in peace.

> *(Choir begins to hum "Dona nobis pacem." Narrators continue speaking over choir, their voices building in both intensity and sincerity.)*

B: The beauty of the words is available to us all—

A & B: we have but to look.

A: The music of the spheres is in our hearts—

A & B: we have but to listen.

B: We can all live in peace—

A & B: we have but to pray.

Dona nobis pacem

Poster by Francesca Martino

Back to the Beatles

Title	Composer/Lyricist
Here Comes the Sun	George Harrison arr. Alan Billingsley
Happy Together	Garry Bonner & Alan Gordon arr. Greg Jasperse
If I Fell in Love with You	John Lennon & Paul McCartney

The rest of the pieces are by Lennon & McCartney; only the arrangers are listed for each piece.

Long and Winding Road	Paul Langford
Penny Lane	Audrey Snyder
Imagine	Mac Huff
Ob-La-Di, Ob-La-Da	Mark Brymer
Let It Be	Mark Brymer
Eleanor Rigby	Roger Emerson
Hey Jude	Deke Sharon
Hello, Goodbye	Alan Billingsley
Yesterday	Mark Brymer
When I'm Sixty-Four	Alan Billingsley
Good Night	Audrey Snyder
All You Need Is Love	Alan Billingsley

Begin with a film clip from the original Ed Sullivan show and share with your audience as the opening. We used the last couple of minutes from the Beatles' movie "Hard Days Night" that we checked out from the local library. Have some girls suddenly run through the aisles and scream for the Beatles, just as it really happened! The screaming section will need little rehearsal, and shouldn't be too long. Wear black pants, black shoes, and white long-sleeved shirts for this performance.

A link to a YouTube video of a program excerpt is available at www.giamusic.com/ccc.

Back to the Beatles

Prologue

Film clip of the Beatles

> *To transition from film to choir, the choir will be positioned to run down aisles into the pit area, re-enacting the greeting given to the Beatles upon their arrival in the United States. (Music: "She Loves You!") The girls will wave autograph books at the Beatles in the film, scream, cry out, pretend to faint, squeal, and jump up and down. At the cue decided upon by the director, they will begin to move up onto the stage and as the film comes to an end, transition from star-struck teeny-boppers into the choir formation required for their first number. Narrator will step forward, open script, and begin the narration.*

Opening

The rock and roll phenomenon known as The Beatles was formed in 1962, just over fifty years ago. Tonight we celebrate their wonderful music with our program "Back to the Beatles." What made the Beatles unique from other musical groups was that they wrote their own songs, they played their own songs, and they used no artificial gimmicks to sell their songs. No indeed, no flares or explosives were necessary for the Beatles! Their focus was strictly on music. Certainly no other group can touch the quality of music the Beatles produced. Agreed, other groups have written a few good songs, but the Beatles wrote more than 100 great songs, including George Harrison's beautiful "Here Comes the Sun."

SECTION 1

The year 1969 was an extremely difficult one for Harrison. He had temporarily quit the band, had had his tonsils removed, and had even been arrested. Also, during that period, Harrison's time was consumed with businessmen and accountants, professionals necessary to his career, but whom he deplored. One day he rebelled and escaped to Eric Clapton's house where he wandered around Clapton's garden, playing an acoustic guitar and writing "Here Comes the Sun." The song celebrates the joy and promise of a new day like none other, a day like one Harrison most fervently hoped would soon be coming to him.

Here Comes the Sun

SECTION 2

Written by Jerry Brown and Alan Gordon, "Happy Together" is one of the most frequently covered songs in radio history. Since 1967 it has had approximately 500 million performances on American radio—it is the forty-fourth most-played song in the USA. Used in a wide variety of TV shows and movies, "Happy Together" has been covered by everyone from Petula Clark to the Red Army choir and, of course, by the Beatles.

Happy Together

SECTION 3

Written primarily by John Lennon, "If I Fell in Love with You" is notable for its unusual structure, which includes an unrepeated introductory section sung by Lennon followed by sequential verse sections, each having a slightly expanded form. The remainder of the song features two-part harmony, sung by Lennon and McCartney at the same microphone, with Lennon singing the lower harmony and McCartney singing the higher one. It is a beautiful song, and we promise you will fall in love with it, just as we have.

If I Fell in Love with You

SECTION 4

Who exactly were the Beatles? Known as "the four lads from Liverpool," the most controversial was the edgy John Lennon, the most diplomatic was Paul McCartney (and the girls also thought he was the cutest!). George Harrison was quiet and withdrawn, while Ringo Starr, who joined the Beatles in Hamburg, Germany, had a good sense of humor and was the most approachable. Like so many other aspiring young British musicians, the four young men formed a band and began to play gigs around Liverpool, England, and Hamburg. It was not an easy life. Pay was poor and a gig could easily last eight hours of nonstop singing. During those formative years, the Beatles suffered many disappointments and setbacks. In light of their phenomenal success, it is perhaps too easy for us to forget that, for them, the road to the top was indeed "The Long and Winding Road."

The Long and Winding Road

SECTION 5

There is a real Penny Lane, you know, a Penny Lane filled with the "blue sunshine of happy memories." "Penny Lane," written by Paul McCartney, is one of the most uplifting and cheery of all the Beatles' songs. It is also the most autobiographical. There really is a bus depot on Penny Lane, a bank on a corner, and a barbershop where pictures are on display of the different haircuts available to customers. The song has a gorgeous melody, with very contemporary arrangements. Added to this is trumpet work by David Mason, whom McCartney heard playing in a BBC production of Bach's *Brandenburg Concerto No. 2*. Mason's trumpet work in "Penny Lane" was the perfect finishing touch for the song, and McCartney was finally satisfied with the results.

Penny Lane

SECTION 6

"Imagine" was the best selling single of John Lennon's career. Inspired by a poem written by Yoko Ono, the song asks the listeners to imagine a world at peace, and for humanity to focus on living lives unattached to material possessions. "Imagine" is one of the 100 most-performed songs of the century and is also listed as one of the top 365 songs of the century in the *Guinness Book of World Records: British Hit Singles and Albums.* It has been covered by such artists as Stevie Wonder, Madonna, Joan Baez, Elton John, and Diana Ross.

Imagine

SECTION 7

"Ob-La-Di, Ob-La-Da" is a lighthearted reggae song intended to be a Beatles single, but both John and George originally rejected it. Paul had to not only convince John and George to do the song, he also had to pay off a local reggae musician who claimed "Ob-La-Di, Ob-La Da" was the name of his reggae band and that Paul must have seen one of his promo posters hanging around town. The musician was in jail for non-payment of child support and Paul, feeling sorry for the guy, agreed to give him 111 British pounds to have him released. The man dutifully paid his child support, signed the title over to Paul, and the Beatles owned "Ob-La-Di, Ob-La-Da."

Ob-La-Di, Ob-La-Da

SECTION 8

One has only to read the newspapers or watch the news on TV to know that the world is a troubled place. It was a troubled place in the 1960s as well, and Paul McCartney, worn out by the turmoil in the world and the increasing tension amongst the Beatles, felt the strain. One night he went to bed totally discouraged, and as he slept, a song came to him. He began writing the next morning, with the first line already intact in his head. "When I find myself in times of trouble Mother Mary comes to me. . . ." In this case, the "Mother Mary" he was referring to was his own mother, Mary McCartney; in his time of need he called to her and she offered solace, assuring him that everything would turn out fine. Through his music, McCartney found peace and then he shared that peace with the rest of the world with his beautiful "Let It Be."

Let It Be

Section 9

"Eleanor Rigby" is a song about lonely people, in this case, a spinster and a priest whose lives do not intersect until her funeral. Paul McCartney claimed the name "Eleanor Rigby" was entirely fictional; but remember: Life is stranger than fiction! In 1980 a gravestone was discovered in the churchyard of St. Peter's Church in Liverpool that bears the name of an actual Eleanor Rigby, and at one time Paul McCartney and John Lennon had met just yards from that gravestone to discuss a current project. Perhaps McCartney had seen the name at that time and subliminally retained it, but who knows for sure? The music for "Eleanor Rigby" was performed entirely by a pair of string quartets, an idea McCartney wasn't too thrilled about until each violin was individually fitted with a microphone that gave "a more biting sound to the music."

Eleanor Rigby

Section 10

Written by Paul McCartney, "Hey Jude" has long been considered as a consolation song to himself, because his long-term relationship with lady-love Jan Aster was ending and the Beatles' future was growing more and more uncertain. It is the longest Beatle song, clocking in at 7 minutes 11 seconds, making it longer than most radios would allow to be played; at that time radio DJs insisted songs be no more than 3 ½ minutes long, so there was a real question as to whether or not "Hey Jude" would even be given air time. The reason the song is so long is that the refrain goes on for a full four minutes, even longer than the verses, because McCartney was having too much fun to quit improvising.

A 36-piece orchestra had been hired, and the classical musicians were encouraged to clap and sing along for double their usual rate of pay. The recording session was a tremendous success, in spite of the fact that Harrison's guitar playing had to be toned down and Ringo Starr nearly missed his opening cue.

Released in 1981, "Hey Jude" spent nine weeks at number 1 on the charts.

Hey Jude

Section 11

"Hello, Goodbye" is bouncy and irresistible. It's basically a simple song of duality. McCartney got the idea for the song while demonstrating to an assistant, Alistair Taylor, how to write a song. Taylor remembers, "He told me to hit any note on the keyboard and he'd do the same. Whenever he shouted out a word, I would shout out the opposite... 'Black' he shouted. 'White' I replied. 'Yes.' 'No.' 'Hello.' 'Goodbye.'"

Hello, Goodbye

Section 12

John Lennon wrote "Yesterday" at age 23. "Yesterday" is considered one of the best songs he wrote during his solo career. The melody came to him in a dream, and when he woke up, he just sat down and wrote the words to the melody. In it Lennon explains his philosophy of life, which is a plea for peace, for world unity, and for people everywhere to live simpler lives.

Yesterday

SECTION 13

McCartney had written a version of this song when he was just sixteen years old. It is assumed he revised and rewrote the number in 1966 as a tribute to his father, who had reached the age of 64 in July of that year. Evidences of his father's musical tastes are evident in the number. The song speaks to the sensitivity of a young Paul McCartney to the process of aging.

"When I'm Sixty-Four" was the first track to be completed for the album *Sgt. Pepper's Lonely Hearts Club Band,* and has been recorded by over 40 different artists around the world.

When I'm Sixty-Four

SECTION 14

"Good Night" was a children's lullaby that John Lennon originally wrote for his five-year-old son, Julian. Ringo was to do the vocals and it was to be featured as the final track on the "The Beatles" double album.

At the initial recording session, Ringo made some brief spoken invitations to the children to settle into bed while he sang them the song. Sadly, this element was dropped from the final version of the song. Also, the original song was to be sung in a very simple way with Lennon backing Ringo's vocals on an acoustic guitar. Eventually a much more lavish production was recorded with an orchestra of 26 musicians as well as an eight-voice choir. How wonderful it would be if both versions of the song were available to us today!

Good Night

SECTION 15

"All You Need Is Love" was written specifically for the *Our World Programme*, which was beamed to over 400 million viewers of Sunday, June 25, 1967. Imagine, in a day that did not have the internet or cell phones, 400 million people from all around the world were able to tune in their TVs and radios at the same time to watch and listen to the same program! It was an amazing first.

All You Need Is Love

Poster by Dan Vogt

The Birds and the Bees

Title	Composer/Lyricist
The Birds and the Bees	Herb Newman
Morning Has Broken	Eleanor Farjeon arr. Harry Simeone
Breakaway	Matthew Gerrard, Avril Lavigne, & Bridget Benenate arr. Teena Chinn
Feed the Birds *Mary Poppins*	Richard M. Sherman & Robert B. Sherman arr. Cristi Cary Miller
Rockin' Robin	Jimmie Thomas arr. Roger Emerson
A Nightingale Sang in Berkeley Square	Manning Sherwin/Eric Maschwitz arr. Alan Billingsley
Bumble Bee	Anders Edenroth
The Turtle Dove	English folk song arr. John Purifoy
Now Is the Month of Maying	Thomas Morley arr. Harry Robert Wilson & Walter Ehret
Blue Skies	Irving Berlin arr. Roger Emerson
Till There Was You *The Music Man*	Meredith Willson arr. Mac Huff
When the Red, Red Robin (Comes Bob, Bob, Bobbin' Along)	Harry Woods arr. Harry Simeone
Blackbird	John Lennon & Paul McCartney arr. Mark Brymer
Blue Moon	Richard Rogers/Lorenz Hart Jay Althouse

Reprise

The Birds and the Bees	Herb Newman

> *A great way to begin a program is with a nice unison song that has a catchy melody performed by all of the singers. Much of this concert lends itself to having movement, especially "Rockin' Robin," "When the Red, Red Robin Comes Bob, Bob, Bobbin' Along," and "Blue Moon." Get into the style of the music!*

The Birds and the Bees

Note 1: This program uses two narrators, A and B. It also includes a violinist, a cellist, and a grand piano. The piano should be preset stage left.

Note 2: Before audience enters, be sure to focus and preset the spot down center for the violinist, making sure its radius is large enough to include the two narrators. You do not want to make any lighting adjustments during the opening moments.

Note 3: Curtains are closed. Choirs quietly enter. Narrators A and B and the violinist go to their places, ready to enter, with the violinist center behind main act curtain, Narrator A stage right, and Narrator B stage left.

House lights slowly dim to out. Two people hold the curtain open and the violinist enters through curtains to center stage, stands quietly a moment and then, in the dark, begins to play the opening section of "The Birds and the Bees," using a slow tempo. As the violinist plays, slowly bring up spot. At predetermined point in the music, Narrator A enters from stage right and Narrator B enters from stage left and they cross to stand in spot on either side of the violinist. They need to be in the light, but should not crowd the musician; they should stand about three steps on either side and slightly in front, forming a shallow triangle. If at all possible, the lines of the poem should be memorized, as the lighting will not be sufficient for reading and because the opening moment should appear effortless with no distractions. If the readers feel they must use a script, then they need to be as uniform as possible in their presentation, opening their binders at the same moment and holding them in the same manner. "A Prayer in Spring" by Robert Frost is to be spoken as written here, rather than in its original quatrain form. This rearrangement for this presentation lends itself to easier oral interpretation. The readers need to rehearse both together and with the music, for the violinist is to continue playing under their words. The music should gently end shortly after the last word of the poem is spoken. The spot should go up on the narrator(s) before they speak at each section and should be out before they move to exit at the end of each narration.

Section I

A: "Oh, give us pleasure in the flowers today;

and give us not to think so far away

as the uncertain harvest;

keep us here all simply in the springing of the year.

B: Oh, give us pleasure in the orchard white,

like nothing else by day,

A: like ghosts by night;

B: and make us happy in the happy bees,

the swarm dilating round the perfect trees.

A: And make us happy in the darting bird that

suddenly above the bees is heard,

B: the meteor that thrusts in with needle bill,

and off a blossom in mid-air stands still.

A: For this is love and nothing else is love,

the which it is reserved for God above

to sanctify to what far ends He will,

A & B: but which it only needs that we fulfill."

Music concludes. Spot down, curtain opens, and general stage lights up. As the audience applauds, the violinist begins to play "The Birds and the Bees" in an up tempo; singers are already on stage or enter at this time, depending on director's choice. Choir should be full of energy and having fun. At this time Narrators A and B move to stage left, where they will work from within the curve of the grand piano for the remainder of the show. Spot will move to that predetermined position and illuminate them at the appropriate times throughout the remainder of the show. Spot should not be on narrators except while they are speaking, but instead smoothly fade up and dim down for the delivery of the transitions. The spot operator should rehearse with the narrators and also have a script, appropriately marked with the required cues. If possible, each narrator should be provided with a microphone. Choir and director will be standing poised and in position on stage, ready to sing, or ready to enter, depending on the choice of the director. Narrators A and B will open their scripts and

> *begin speaking only* after *"The Birds and the Bees" has been sung and the next song is ready to be introduced.*

The Birds and the Bees

SECTION 2

B: Popularized by singer Cat Stevens, the lyrics of "Morning has Broken" were written by English poet and children's author Eleanor Farjeon. Asked to write a song in praise of the Creator and to celebrate new beginnings, Farjeon based her lyrics on Psalm 118, verse 24, which reads,

A: "This is the day which the Lord has made, we will rejoice in it and be glad."

Morning Has Broken

SECTION 3

A: Recorded in 2004 by Kelly Clarkson for *The Princess Diaries 2: The Broken Engagement*, "Breakaway" has been a runaway musical hit.

B: It's a song of courage, for it tells us to spread our wings, to learn how to fly, and to do what it takes to touch the sky.

A: We are to take a risk, take a chance, make a change—

A & B: and break away.

Breakaway

SECTION 4

A: "Feed the Birds" was written in 1964 by Richard and Robert Sherman for the Walt Disney production of *Mary Poppins*.

B: Sung at a reverent tempo, the song has definite religious overtones.

B: "Feed the Birds" was reputedly Walt Disney's favorite song, and after work on Friday nights, Disney would often invite the Sherman brothers into his office to talk about how things were going at the studio. After a while, Disney would saunter over to the window in his office, look out into the distance, and just say, "Play it."

A: And Dick Sherman would go to the piano and play "Feed the Birds." One time, just as he was almost finished, his brother Robert heard Walt say, "Yep. That's what it's all about."

Feed the Birds

Section 5

B: Written by Leon Rene under the pseudonym of Jimmie Thomas and first recorded by Bobby Day, "Rockin' Robin" is a rock and roll list of all the little birds on J-Bird Street.

A: It is perhaps best remembered for the 1972 version recorded and released by a very young and very talented Michael Jackson.

Rockin' Robin

Section 6

B: Berkeley Square is a large leafy square in Mayfair, which is an expensive part of London. The resident birds, stimulated by the streetlights, can often be heard singing at night.

A: Published in 1940, early in World War II, "A Nightingale Sang in Berkeley Square" has subsequently become a standard, recorded by everyone from Frank Sinatra to Nat King Cole to The Manhattan Transfer.

A Nightingale Sang in Berkeley Square

Section 7

A: *(Taking a step forward)* Humble: modest, unassuming in attitude, behavior and feeling. Showing respect.

B: *(Taking a step forward)* Bumblebee: Any number of related large hairy, yellow and black social bees. Like the honeybees, the bumblebees feed on nectar and gather pollen.

A: Though not true for all, most bumblebee species are gentle.

B: From this comes their original name—

A: "humble bee." *(A and B step back)*

Bumble Bee

SECTION 8

A: Dating from eighteenth-century Dorset, England, "The Turtle Dove" is a traditional British folk song.

B: "Fare you well, my dear," it says, "I must be gone, and leave you for awhile;

A: If I roam away I'll come back again, though I roam ten thousand miles, my dear, though I roam ten thousand miles."

The Turtle Dove

SECTION 9

A: Written in 1595 by Thomas Morley, "Now Is the Month of Maying" is one of the most famous of English madrigals. Morley, a Renaissance composer, theorist, and foremost member of the composers known as the English madrigal school, was also organist at St. Paul's Cathedral.

B: For a time Morley lived in the same parish as William Shakespeare, and while a connection between the two has long been speculated, it has, regretfully, never been proven.

Now Is the Month of Maying

SECTION 10

A: Written by Irving Berlin in 1926, "Blue Skies" was first sung in the musical *Betsy* in New York City and was an instant hit.

B: Numerous recording stars have used it since, from Bing Crosby in the 1946 movie *Blue Skies* to Count Basie, Benny Goodman, Willie Nelson, Jim Reeves, and Thelonious Monk.

A: The "bluebird of happiness" is a symbol of cheer. You hear "bluebird singing a song—nothing but bluebirds all day long."

B: This song optimistically focuses on love and the beauties of nature—birds singing, the sun shining, and of course blue skies.

Blue Skies

SECTION 11

A: In 1957 an amazing musical titled *The Music Man* opened on Broadway. Counted among its plethora of wonderful songs by Meredith Willson is a love song sung by librarian Marian Paroo to Professor Harold Hill. The song Marian sings so beautifully is "Till There Was You."

B: *The Music Man* became a Broadway hit, winning five Tony awards, including Best Musical, and ran for an astounding 1,375 performances.

Till There Was You

SECTION 12

(This selection may need to be omitted unless it is sung in unison. This arrangement is currently out of print and there is not another recommended substitute. However, a unison version can be purchased.)

A: "When the Red, Red Robin (Comes Bob, Bob, Bobbin' Along)" was a popular song written in 1926 by Harry M. Woods. It's had a lot of success down through the years!

B: Al Jolson achieved a triumph with his recording of the song when his rendition reached number 1 on the charts.

A: Lillian Roth sang it during the height of her musical career.

B: And Doris Day did it again in 1953.

A: Finally, the song achieved fame in another way when it helped inspire the name of a popular casual dining restaurant chain called "Red Robin."

B: It seems the owner of the original Red Robin restaurant sang in a barbershop quartet who frequently sang the song. He liked the song, and so. . .

A: Anybody for a hamburger?

When the Red, Red Robin (Comes Bob, Bob, Bobbin' Along)

SECTION 13

A: We all know the Beatles.

B: We all know the famous White Album.

A: But do you know that the famous song "Blackbird" with its guitar accompaniment was inspired by Johann Sebastian Bach's "Bourrée in E Minor"?

B: "Bourrée in E Minor" is a well-known lute piece that is often played on the classical guitar.

A: As children, Paul McCartney and George Harrison had to learn it as a "show off" piece, and they never forgot it. They discovered another song was needed for The White Album. . .

B: and so we have the Beatles' beautiful "Blackbird."

Blackbird

SECTION 14

A: Written by Rogers and Hart in 1934, the lyrics of "Blue Moon" refer to an English expression: "once in a blue moon," which means "only very rarely."

B: Mel Tormé sang the song in 1949.

A: And Elvis Presley covered the song in 1956, which was the first crossover recording to rock and roll.

B: The Marcels, a doo-wap group in 1961, also recorded "Blue Moon," and it is they who added the now famous introduction.

Blue Moon

SECTION 15

B: With lyrics by Herb Newman and a song made popular by crooner Dean Martin, "The Birds and the Bees" reminds us about springtime—

A: "the birds and the bees, the flowers and the trees—

B: the moon up above, and best of all—

A & B: a thing called love."

The Birds and the Bees

Note: The poem in Section 1—"A Prayer in Spring"—is by Robert Frost.

Poster by Dan Vogt

Moments from Musicals

Title	Composer/Lyricist
Tonight *West Side Story*	Leonard Bernstein/Stephen Sondheim arr. William Stickles
Castle on a Cloud *Les Miserables*	Claude-Michel Schonberg/ Herbert Kretzmer arr. Linda Spevacek
Not While I'm Around *Sweeney Todd*	Stephen Sondheim arr. Mark Brymer
Singin' in the Rain *Singin' in the Rain*	Nacio Herb Brown/Arthur Freed arr. Ruth Elaine Schram
Never Never Land *Peter Pan*	Jule Styne/Betty Comden & Adolph Green arr. Mac Huff
Try to Remember *The Fantasticks*	Harvey Schmidt/Tom Jones arr. Jay Althouse
Summertime *Porgy and Bess*	George Gershwin/ Dubose Heyward & Ira Gershwin arr. Mark Hayes
And All That Jazz *Chicago*	John Kander/Fred Ebb arr. Kirby Shaw
Memory *Cats*	Andrew Lloyd-Webber/T. S. Eliot arr. Ed Lojeski
Ain't Misbehavin' *Ain't Misbehavin'*	Thomas "Fats" Waller & Harry Brooks/Andy Razaf arr. Larry Shackley
Over the Rainbow *The Wizard of Oz*	Harold Arlen/Edgar "Yip" Harburg arr. Russell Robinson
Wouldn't It Be Loverly? *My Fair Lady*	Frederick Loewe/Alan Jay Lerner arr. Robert H. Noelte
Home *The Wiz*	Charlie Smalls arr. Andy Beck and Michael Spresser
Shine *Billy Elliot*	Elton John/Lee Hall arr. Mark Brymer

'S Wonderful George Gershwin/
Funny Face Ira Gershwin
out of print arr. Clay Warnick
alternate arrangement arr. Russell Robinson

Forget About the Boy Jeanine Tesori/Dick Scanlan
Thoroughly Modern Millie arr. Audrey Snyder

You Can't Stop the Beat Marc Shaiman/Marc Shaiman &
Hairspray Scott Wittman
 arr. Roger Emerson

Moments from Musicals will need to include choreography. "Singin' in the Rain" looks great with some umbrellas. Do you have tap dancers? Everyone can add a shuffle step or two when you sing "Forget About the Boy." The closing number has to be performed with energy, so that's why "You Can't Stop the Beat" is a great choice. Fun movement is the show's style, so perhaps invest in a choreographer.

There are also many types of props and accessories that can enhance this performance. Consider using some of these:

- *Headbands with a flower pinned center front*
- *Long strings of beads to twirl (perhaps pop-it beads)*
- *Bowler hats*
- *Yellow umbrellas*
- *White gloves*
- *Shiny silver gloves that sparkle*
- *Rainbow scarves or scarves with each one of a solid rainbow color*

A link to a YouTube video of a program excerpt is available at www.giamusic.com/ccc.

Moments from Musicals

> *This program calls for the use of one narrator, who reads the text printed below before each piece in this program.*

Section 1

> *When the auditorium is dark and quiet, we should hear the choir humming the opening bars of "Tonight." As the choir hums, the main act curtain opens slowly and quietly, and lights gradually come up. Only when the curtain is fully open and the stage is completely lit does the choir begin to sing the actual words to the song. This opening needs to be rehearsed so all is coordinated and smooth. Otherwise, the opening, structured to be gentle and to ease us into a nostalgic frame of mind, will fall flat. Soloist begins and choir joins at the repeat.*

Tonight

Section 2

Leonard Bernstein's tender love song, "Tonight," is one of musical theater's most magical moments. I'm sure we all remember when we first heard this soaring duet sung by two young people, who, in spite of the odds against them, fall deeply and tragically in love. "Tonight" is indeed the appropriate song to open this evening's performance, for tonight we are celebrating just such glorious moments in musical theater history when a seminal song, a rapturous lyric, or a tender word touched our souls and forever became an integral part of our personal lives.

Besides "Tonight" from *West Side Story*, nowhere else does this connection become more evident than with the beautiful "Castle on a Cloud" from *Les Miserables*.

> *(Soloist moves slowly forward to stand slightly off narrator's left shoulder.)*

The song is a dream—a dream sung by a wistful, yearning child. Can dreams come true? Yes, they can, according to composer Claude

Michael Schoenberg, and not only for little Cosette, but also for us. As we listen to Cosette sing, her dream becomes ours and perhaps—at a magical moment—the dreams join and travel together to little Cosette's beautiful castle on a cloud.

> *(Narrator closes script and exits right;* soloist *steps forward and begins song.)*

Soloist: Castle on a Cloud

Section 3

Known for his lyrical wit, somber tone, and uncompromising dedication to his own artistic ideals, Stephen Sondheim's most successful musical appeared in 1979. *Sweeney Todd* is Sondheim at his darkest—and his most melodious. The first song sets the tone for the entire show, which has proven to be both terrifying—and funny. Sweeney Todd, the mad barber, returns from an unjust imprisonment, determined to get back at the world. Mrs. Lovett becomes his accomplice in murder, helping him turn corpses into meat pies. Grisly as the subject matter is, we can still identify with the frustration and anger that sweeps over us when we are accused of doing something of which we are entirely innocent.

Not While I'm Around

Section 4

The stage is dark. Audience anticipation is high. Will it truly rain on stage, as the advertisements have promised? Will it be real water, or just a silver rain curtain? And heavens! What happens if the people in the front rows get wet? The lights come up—the rain comes down—and how wonderful! It is real water! It is actually raining on stage! And that water is kicked with abandon, happily splashed in, and yes, the people in the front row do get just a little bit wet! No one minds, however, for there can be no more joyous celebration of life and love, and yes, even of rain, than the jubilant musical *Singin' in the Rain*.

Singin' in the Rain

SECTION 5

Never has there been more magic on stage than in the adaptation of J. M. Barrie's *Peter Pan*. There's naughty little Tinkerbelle's fairy dust; Wendy, John, and Michael discovering they can fly; and after an uproarious battle on a pirate ship between nasty pirates and a ragtag bunch of Lost Boys, we hear the "tick-tock, tick-tock" of an ever-hungry alligator. When the delightful song "Never Never Land" is sung in Act I, Peter makes a promise to Wendy that as long as there are children and as long as those children have imaginations, magical islands really can exist. Best of all, Peter tells Wendy, Never Never Land is a place where people can remain children forever and no one need ever grow old. To never grow up, Peter explains, is the best magic in the world!

Never Never Land

SECTION 6

On May 3, 1960, the longest-running musical in theater history opened at the tiny 150-seat Sullivan Street Playhouse in Greenwich Village, remaining there for 40 years. Everything about *The Fantasticks* is intimate: the orchestra consists of no more than a harp and a piano, the cast is only eight people, and the audience is so close to the stage that it feels part of the action. Let us now "try to remember," as the song instructs us, "the kind of September when life was slow and oh, so mellow, try to remember, and if you can remember, then follow, follow, follow, follow."

Try to Remember

SECTION 7

If any one person can be said to be the musical soul of the 1920s, it is George Gershwin. Thrilled by the new sound of jazz, Gershwin introduced those jazz ideas into his theater work, and so impressed the American elite that he caused them to reverse their previous negative attitudes toward this heretofore-despised musical form. However, when *Porgy and Bess* debuted in 1935, the critics, totally confused by its form, continued to be antagonistic and dismissed the new production, claiming it was neither a musical nor an opera. It was not a musical, they said, because its main characters were too low class, and it also had far too much singing in it. Neither could it be considered an opera, as Gershwin maintained it was, for it contained too many hit songs. Ah, those critics. If only they could have looked into the future and realized that they were experiencing something entirely new, that *Porgy and Bess* belonged in a category all of its own, where it would eventually be joined by such seminal musicals as *Les Miserables* and *Miss Saigon.*

Summertime

SECTION 8

Chicago is a compelling musical set in Prohibition-era Chicago. Written by John Kander and Fred Ebb and choreographed by Bob Fosse, the approach of *Chicago* is a definite bow to the music and style of the 1920s. The story is a satire on both corruption in the administration of criminal justice, and on the "celebrity criminal," a concept that we are quite used to today. In an attempt to add verisimilitude to th stage production, many of the songs are deliberate takeoffs on classic vaudeville pieces that had been performed during the 1920s. This is nowhere more evident than with the Fosse classic, "And All That Jazz."

And All That Jazz

SECTION 9

Written by Andrew Lloyd-Webber, the ever-popular musical *Cats* is based on T. S. Eliot's book of poems, *Old Possum's Book of Practical Cats*. *Cats* is representative of a genre of musicals introduced during the final years of the twentieth century; these new musicals were called "concept musicals." A concept musical need not have a plot at all, though it may have the thread of one. Indeed, a concept musical is actually more like a revue, but one with a serious rather than comedic theme. In *Cats* the theme is exemplified by a scruffy, abused, and completely hopeless little feline named Grizabella, the Glamour Cat. It is Grizabella who is eventually chosen by all the other Jellicle cats to ascend to the Heavyside Layer and return with a new life. As she ascends to the Heavyside Layer, Grizabella sings the hauntingly beautiful "Memory," a song which is introduced when Grizabella first appears early in Act I.

> *Either the choir or a soloist may sing "Memory."*

Memory

SECTION 10

Ain't Misbehavin' is a musical revue that is a tribute to the black musicians of the 1920s and '30s. These musicians were part of the Harlem Renaissance—an era of growing black creativity, cultural awareness, and ethnic pride. It was a time when Manhattan nightclubs such as the Cotton Club and the Savoy Ballroom were the playgrounds of high society, and pianists were banging out the new beat known as "swing." Recorded by such notables as Louis Armstrong and Ella Fitzgerald, the song "Ain't Misbehavin'" reflects composer Fats Waller's view of life as a journey meant for pleasure and play.

Ain't Misbehavin'

SECTION 11

Beginnings of musicals are always supposed to create suspense; they make us want to know where the show will take us. If the opening does not get the audience's attention, the show's chances of success are slim. Therefore, the opening moments of a performance are of vital importance, for that is where the tone of the show is established and its atmosphere, concerns, and musical style are set. As a result of this line of thinking, one of the most popular songs in all of musical theater history was nearly cut from its original script. "Over the Rainbow" was a ballad placed early in the iconic *The Wizard of Oz,* and was sung by a rather sad and wistful Dorothy. The producers were horrified. They considered the song too slow, too mournful, and totally misplaced. Cut it, they advised, cut it immediately. *(Short pause and then a little smile.)* Aren't we glad they didn't?

Over the Rainbow

SECTION 12

One of the most popular of all musicals is *My Fair Lady.* Except for the radical alteration of having Henry Higgins fall in love with Eliza Doolittle—something the character does not do in *Pygmalion,* the original play by George Bernard Shaw—Allen Jay Lerner's libretto remains carefully centered on Shaw's work. Another reason for the phenomenal success of the show is that Lerner employed subtle changes in language for his lyrics, and, depending on who was singing, made the songs an actual extension of the characters. As a result, we have "Wouldn't It Be Loverly?" in a Cockney accent, sung by Eliza as she dreams of a better life than that of being a simple flower seller in London. Later on, also sung by Eliza, we hear the perfectly articulated song "The Rain in Spain." Here is the delightful "Wouldn't It Be Loverly?" It's the epitome of all dream songs ever sung by a young woman.

Wouldn't It Be Loverly?

SECTION 13

In 1975 another adaptation of Frank L. Baum's book, *The Wonderful Wizard of Oz*, opened in a theater in Baltimore, Maryland. Entitled *The Wiz*, it was a retelling of the popular classic within the context of the African American culture. With a rock score and a decidedly modern libretto, *The Wiz* reframes the old, familiar story into something more relevant to today's modern audiences. Thus we have such songs as "Ease On Down the Road," "Slide Some Oil to Me," and "Don't Nobody Bring Me No Bad News." One of the final songs Dorothy sings in *The Wiz* is "Home," where she thinks about what she has learned, gained, and lost on her journey to Oz and back again. "When I think of home," Dorothy sings, "I think of a place where there's love overflowing. I wish I was home, I wish I was back there—." Then she clicks her silver slippers and is instantly transported home. For all of us here this evening, home means that to us, too. Home is a place where there is always "love overflowing."

Home

SECTION 14

It is part of human nature to want to shine in something we do. In fact, some of us are passionate enough about what we want to actually achieve greatness, whether it is in the field of sports, art, music, or dance. In *Billy Elliot the Musical* the lead character, Billy, is a talented young boy in England who discovers an unexpected love of dance. Set against a bitter year-long coal strike and the gradual disintegration of his family, Billy struggles to achieve his dream. A 2009 Tony Award winner for Best Musical, Best Book, Best Score, and Best Choreography, *Billy Elliot* teaches us all valuable lessons in tolerance and acceptance.

Shine

SECTION 15

In 1957 an American film titled *Funny Face*, featuring the music of George and Ira Gershwin, was released to an enthusiastic public. Starring Audrey Hepburn and Fred Astaire, the story is a romance between two people from very different walks of life. Astaire, a professional photographer, is desperately seeking a new look for the fall fashion collection. Hepburn is an intellectual bookstore owner who disparages high fashion as "chichi." However, Astaire soon discovers that Hepburn is not only the girl he wants to photograph, but she is also the girl with whom he is falling in love. And that love, as both characters eventually discover, is "'S Wonderful."

'S Wonderful

SECTION 16

Thoroughly Modern Millie, based on the 1957 Julie Andrews film, brings lightness and cheer back to Broadway. After a decade of well-crafted but dark musicals, the first years of the twenty-first century had the audiences once again exiting the theaters whistling and smiling. *Thoroughly Modern Millie* is a delightfully frivolous musical centered on marriage, romance, and a diabolical scheme to sell young girls into slavery. The producers of the show wished to do no more than entertain their audiences, a goal they easily accomplished with flapper era costumes, fun songs, and energetic tap dancing. Nowhere are these three components more apparent than in the song "Forget About the Boy," sung by Millie as she tries to persuade herself to marry her rich boss and forget about Jimmy, her one true love.

Forget About the Boy

SECTION 17

Set in 1962 in Baltimore, Maryland, *Hairspray* follows the "pleasingly plump" Tracy Turnblad as she pursues stardom as a dancer on a local TV show and rallies against racial segregation. The determined Tracy, who says anyone who loves to dance should be allowed to do so, is easy for all of us to identify with. For those of us who love to sing, who cannot help but listen to music whenever possible, and who have acquired a stockpile of musical moments that have become woven into the very fabric of our lives, we understand Tracy Turnblad completely. We share her triumphs as well as her view for the future as we join together to sing "You Can't Stop the Beat."

You Can't Stop the Beat

Trinity High School Spring Fine Arts Show

Musical Conversations

Tuesday, May 12th

Featuring Bel Coro, Chamber Choir, Le Ragazze, the Instrumental Ensemble, and our student artists' recent work.

Welcoming St Patrick's Men's Choir

6:30 gallery opening
7:00 choral concert

Reception immediately following

Trinity High School Auditorium

Poster by Dana Nolan

Musical Conversations

Title	Composer/Lyricist
If Music Be the Food of Love	Andy Beck/William Shakespeare
The Tell-Tale Heart *out of print*	Edna Lewis & John Mitri Habash/ Edgar Allan Poe arr. John Mitri Habash
alternate selection The Raven Watches Me	John Parker & Vicki Tucker Courtney text inspired by Edgar Allan Poe
Jonah	Rollo Dilworth
Crossing the Bar	Gwyneth Walker/Alfred Lord Tennyson
Windy Nights	Cynthia Gray/Robert Louis Stevenson
The River Sleeps beneath the Sky	Mary Lynn Lightfoot/ Paul Laurence Dunbar
Route 66	Bobby Troup arr. Roger Emerson
Summertime *Porgy and Bess*	George Gershwin/DuBose Heyward & Ira Gershwin arr. Mark Hayes
If I Can Stop One Heart from Breaking	Paulette Meier/Emily Dickinson arr. Steven Kupferschmid
Won't You Join the Dance? *Alice in Wonderland*	Neil Ginsberg/Lewis Carroll
Barter	René Clausen/Sara Teasdale
A Midsummer Night's Dream	Felix Mendelssohn/ William Shakespeare arr. Emily Crocker
I Dream a World	Rollo Dilworth/Langston Hughes
Master of Music *(closing poem)*	Henry Van Dyke

> *The musical conversation in this concert is between the spoken poetry and the choral pieces. All of the words need to be understood, whether they are spoken or sung. Also do something silly with "Won't You Join the Dance?" These are funny lyrics, so use some funny movements. The closing is a reading that makes a refreshing change for the end of concert. It should be memorized and recited by the entire choir.*

Musical Conversations

> *There are two narrators for this program: Narrator A and Narrator B. Establish Narrator A downstage right and B downstage left. The narrators can speak either from hard black binders or have their script set on a music stand. They will be reading from a variety of genres, from poetry to monologues to selections from short stories. It will be necessary for the narrators to rehearse separately as well as with the choir. The narrators are not to give the source of the readings during the performance. Instead, the sources should be listed on a specific page in the program. The page can be entitled "The Readings for this Program are from the Following Sources" and then the list of the readings should be given in the order of their use in the show.*

SECTION 1

A: *"Twelfth Night"*

If music be the food of love, play on;

Give me excess of it, that, surfeiting,

The appetite may sicken, and so die.

That strain again! It had a dying fall:

O, it came o'er my ear like the sweet sound,

That breathes upon a bank of violets,

Stealing and giving odor! Enough; no more:

'Tis not so sweet as it was before.

O spirit of love! how quick and fresh art thou,

That notwithstanding thy capacity

Receiveth as the sea naught enters there,

Of what validity and pitch soe'er

But falls into abatement and low price,

Even in a minute: so full of shapes is fancy

That it alone is high fantastical.

If Music Be the Food of Love

SECTION 2

B: *"The Tell-Tale Heart"*

No doubt I now grew very pale: but I talked more fluently, and with a heightened voice. Yet the sound increased—and what could I do? It was a low, dull, quick sound—much such a sound as a watch makes when enveloped in cotton. I gasped for breath—and yet the officers heard it not. I talked more quickly—more vehemently; but the noise steadily increased. Oh, God! what could I do? I foamed—I raved—I swore! I swung the chair upon which I had been sitting, and grated it upon the boards, but the noise arose over all and continually increased. It grew louder—louder—louder!

The Tell-Tale Heart

SECTION 3

A: Stories from the Bible were also used as a source for spirituals.

B: For example, the story of Jonah tells the short but poignant tale of three days and three nights in the belly of a giant fish that changed a man forever.

A: Refusing to obey, Jonah ran from God, was tossed from a storm-riddled ship and swallowed by a giant fish God had created especially for that purpose.

B: Jonah was changed forever, and after learning obedience, willingness of spirit, gratitude, and patience, was "spewed forth" from that giant fish and set free, thus ending one of the strangest tales told in the Bible.

A: The men and women first singing Jonah's story hoped they, too, would be "spewed forth" from the "giant fish of slavery" and thus be able to spend the rest of their days living in freedom.

MUSICAL CONVERSATIONS

Jonah

SECTION 4

A: "*Crossing the Bar*"

>Sunset and evening star,
>And one clear call for me!
>And may there be no moaning of the bar,
>When I put out to sea,
>
>But such a tide as moving seems asleep,
>Too full for sound and foam,
>When that which drew from out the boundless deep
>Turns again home.
>
>Twilight and evening bell,
>And after that the dark!
>And may there be no sadness of farewell,
>When I embark;
>
>For though from out our bourn of Time and Place
>The flood may bear me far,
>I hope to see my Pilot face to face
>When I have crost the bar.

Crossing the Bar

SECTION 5

B: "*Windy Nights*"

>Whenever the moon and stars are set,
>Whenever the wind is high,
>All night long in the dark and wet,
>A man goes riding by.

Late in the night when the fires are out,
Why does he gallop and gallop about?

Whenever the trees are crying aloud,
And ships are tossed at sea,
By, on the highway, low and loud,
By at the gallop goes he.
By at the gallop he goes, and then,
By he comes back at the gallop again.

Windy Nights

SECTION 6

A: *"Sunset"*

    The river sleeps beneath the sky,
    And clasps the shadows to its breast:
    The crescent moon shines dim on high;
    And in the lately radiant west
    The gold is fading into gray.
    Now stills the lark his festive lay
    And mourns with me the dying day.

    While in the south the first faint star
    Lifts to the night its silver face,
    And twinkles to the moon afar
    Across the heaven's graying space,
    Low murmurs reach me from the town,
    As Day puts on her somber crown,
    And shakes her mantle darkly down.

The River Sleeps beneath the Sky

Section 7

B: *"Summer in the South"*

> The oriole sings in the greening grove
> As if he were half-way waiting,
> The rosebuds peep from their hoods of green,
> Timid and hesitating.
> The rain comes down in a torrent sweep
> And the nights smell warm and piney,
> The garden thrives, but the tender shoots
> Are yellow-green and tiny.
> Then a flash of sun on a waiting hill,
> Streams laugh that erst were quiet,
> The sky smiles down with a dazzling blue
> And the woods run mad with riot.

Summertime

Section 8

A: *"If I Can Stop One Heart From Breaking"*

> If I can stop one heart from breaking,
> I shall not live in vain;
> If I can ease one life the aching,
> Or cool one pain,
> Or help one fainting robin,
> Unto his nest again,
> I shall not live in vain.

If I Can Stop One Heart from Breaking

SECTION 9

B: *"Alice's Adventures in Wonderland"*

"You may not have lived much under the sea—and perhaps you were never even introduced to a lobster—so you can have no idea what a delightful thing a Lobster Quadrille is!"

"It must be a very pretty dance," said Alice timidly.

"Would you like to see a little of it?" said the Mock Turtle.

"Very much indeed," said Alice.

So they began solemnly dancing round and round Alice, every now and then treading on her toes when they passed too close, and waving their forepaws to mark the time.

Won't You Join the Dance?

SECTION 10

A: *"Barter"*

>   Life has loveliness to sell,
>   All beautiful and splendid things,
>   Blue waves whitened on a cliff,
>   Soaring fire that sways and sings,
>   And children's faces looking up
>   Holding wonder like a cup.

>   Life has loveliness to sell,
>   Scent of pine trees in the rain,
>   Eyes that love you, arms that hold,
>   And for your spirit's still delight,
>   Holy thoughts that star the night.

Spend all you have for loveliness,

Buy it and never count the cost;

For one white singing hour of peace

Count many a year of strife well lost,

And for a breath of ecstasy

Give all you have been, or could be.

Barter

Section II

B: *"A Midsummer's Night Dream"*

    Over hill, over dale,

    Through brush, through brier,

    Over park, over pale,

    Through flood, through fire.

    I do wander everywhere,

    Swifter than the moon's sphere;

    And I serve the fairy queen,

    To dew her orbs upon the green.

    The cowslips tall her pensioners be:

    In their gold coats spots you see;

    Those be rubies, fairy favors,

    In those freckles live their savors.

    I must go seek some dewdrops here

    And hang a pearl in every cowslip's ear.

        Farewell, thou lob of spirits, I'll be gone.

        Our queen and our elves come here anon.

A Midsummer Night's Dream

Section 12

A: "I Dream a World..."

> *The musical lyrics and poetry have been tied together throughout "Musical Conversations." This final piece of music will be one powerfully combined set of the same lyrics and music. The text for "I Dream a World" is printed in the music. Narrator A begins at measure 14 with "I dream a world where man...." Continue with the second verse. Narrator A & B should alternate phrases of the lyrics and use the same dynamics with their voices as indicated in the music. They should conclude in unison and with "I Dream a World" (at measure 37).*

I Dream a World

Closing

Section 13

"Master of Music" should be memorized and recited in unison by the whole choir (or choirs).

Master of Music

by Henry Van Dyke

Glory of architect, glory of painter, and sculptor, and bard,
Living forever in temple and picture and statue and song, —
Look how the world with the lights that they lit
    is illumined and starred,
Brief was the flame of their life, but the lamps of their art burn long!

Where is the Master of Music, and how has he vanished away?
Where is the work that he wrought with his wonderful art in the air?
Gone, — it is gone like the glow on the cloud at the close of the day!
The Master has finished his work, and the glory of music is —where?

Once, at the wave of his wand, all the billows of musical sound
Followed his will, as the sea was ruled by the prophet of old:
Now that his hand is relaxed, and his rod has dropped to the ground,
Silent and dark are the shores where the marvelous harmonies rolled!

Nay, but not silent the hearts that were filled by that life-giving sea;
Deeper and purer forever the tides of their being will roll,
Grateful and joyful, O Master, because they have listened to thee, —
The glory of music endures in the depths of the human soul.

> The readings used for this program:
>
> William Shakespeare: *Twelfth Night*
> Edgar Allan Poe: *The Tell-Tale Heart*
> Alfred Lord Tennyson: *Crossing the Bar*
> Robert Louis Stevenson: *Windy Nights*
> Paul Dunbar: *Sunset*
> Paul Dunbar: *Summer in the South*
> Emily Dickenson: *If I Can Stop One Heart from Breaking*
> Lewis Carroll: *Alice's Adventures in Wonderland*
> Sara Teasdale: *Barter*
> William Shakespeare: *A Midsummer Night's Dream*
> Langston Hughes: *I Dream A World*
> Henry Van Dyke: *Master of Music*

Poster by Dana Nolan

The Spirit Says SING!

Title	Composer/Lyricist
How Can I Keep from Singing?	Robert Lowry arr. Andy Beck
Hush! Somebody's Callin' My Name	Traditional spiritual arr. Brazeal W. Dennard
Hole in the Bucket *out of print*	American folk song arr. J. Stanley Sheppard & Brooks Jones
alternate selection Poor Wayfaring Stranger	American folk song arr. Keith Christopher
Crawdad Hole	American folk song arr. Mary Goetze
The Little Horses	Appalachian folk song/ adapt. Aaron Copland arr. Raymond Wilding-White
Mister Sandman	Pat Ballard arr. Ed Lojeski

Simple Gifts
   out of print
   alternate arrangements
	Shaker tune
	arr. Theron Kirk
	arr. Jay Althouse; Julie Wheeler

Ain'-a That Good News!	Traditional spiritual arr. William L. Dawson
Parsley, Sage, Rosemary, and Thyme	English folk song arr. John Coates, Jr.
I'm Gonna Sing When the Spirit Says Sing	Traditional spiritual arr. Howard Helvey

This is a nice occasion to include some American instruments: banjo, fiddle, acoustic guitar, or spoons? It's pretty hard to stand still and sing many of these pieces. Simple choreography can add a lot of energy to pieces such as "Hole in the Bucket" or "I'm Gonna Sing When the Spirit Says Sing."

The Spirit Says SING!

> *In addition to the choir(s), three narrators are also required for this program. Narrators A, B, and C can be placed anywhere on stage the director deems appropriate, though they should remain a group of three so they can interrelate whenever possible. Also, the narrators should remain on stage throughout the entire performance, either standing quietly or sitting on stools during the singing so as to not pull focus away from the choir. They should always stand for the delivery of each section of lines. The spot comes up on the narrators before speaking, so the spot operator needs a cued script and rehearsals so they are not searching for the speaker's stage location.*
>
> *Note 1: While the names of the authors of specific quotes are included here in the script, the author's names are not to be delivered by the narrators during the actual performance. Instead, the author's names should be listed in a separate section of the program dedicated to that specific purpose.*
>
> *Note 2: This program originally included a banjo interlude. The director may keep that interlude, cut it, or replace it with an interlude featuring another instrument of choice. If another instrument is used, then the player's remarks must be changed accordingly to those appropriate to the instrument. Either the musician may give those remarks or Narrator C can deliver them. For the purposes of the continuity of this program, both the instrument and the choice of music should be representative of Appalachia.*

SECTION I

A: "Whenever I hear music, I fear no danger. I am invulnerable, I see no foe. I am related to the earliest of times, and to the latest." *(Henry David Thoreau)*

B: "Music expresses that which cannot be put into words and that which cannot remain silent." *(Victor Hugo)*

C: Singing is the essence of our being, of our human experience. Song unites us.

How Can I Keep from Singing?

Section 2

A: "By borrowing from hymns, reworking them, and then making up new melodies and harmonies, spirituals became the first authentically American sacred music." *(from www.projectmusicworks.org)*

B: The song "Hush, Somebody's Callin' My Name" is one of the greatest, most glorious spirituals of all time. The music makes us feel as though we are being called—at least by the soul of the music, if not by the soul of God." *(Doug Bailey)*

Hush! Somebody's Callin' My Name

Section 3

Option 1

A: And the humor found in folk music is perhaps best represented by Liza, dear Liza and Henry, dear Henry and. . . .

B: A bucket with a hole in it!

C: Wait a minute! A bucket with a hole in it! That doesn't make any sense!

A: That's just what Henry said!

C: And who's this Eliza person?

B: Henry's girlfriend!

C: Oh my goodness, I'm so confused! Who's Henry?

Hole in the Bucket

Option 2

A: Originating in the southern Appalachian mountains during the American Revolution, "Poor Wayfaring Stranger" is a tremendously popular, timeless song.

B: "Poor Wayfaring Stranger" is typical of many of the spirituals of the time expressing the pain and hardship of daily life, while the singer dreams and hopes for a bright and beautiful life after death.

C: We each are always looking for the way to be goin' over home. *(Steve Rouse)*

Poor Wayfaring Stranger

SECTION 4

A: "Appalachia is still, for many American musicians, a kind of fountain of youth they always go back to. . .

B: it's the old home place for a group of artists who represent the quintessence of American independence, fortitude, genius. . .

C: and madness." *(Paul Burch)*

B: Madness? Perhaps, but more than that, humor, and just plain fun!

Crawdad Hole

Interlude—Banjo or other Appalachian instrument

BANJO PLAYER: *(Prior to playing)* Hundreds of articles have been written on the subject of banjos, but one fact most agree on: America's favorite instrument was brought to this country from Africa and Jamaica by slaves in the eighteenth century. *(Additional remarks can be included here; modify the remarks if a different instrument is used.)*

SECTION 5

A: Lullabies are simple expressions of our life experience.

B: They are the songs we hear first.

C: Aaron Copland's *Little Horses* is a lullaby sung by a black wet nurse to a white baby.

A: While she is nursing the white baby, her own child lies hungry and neglected,

C: "So she pours out the liquid music of her voice to quench the thirst of her spirit." *(Nathaniel Hawthorne)*

Little Horses

SECTION 6

Option 1

A: What is more wonderful than the ideal man?

B: Ah . . . but what if we cannot get that perfect fellow in real life?

B: Alright then, what about while we sleep? We can certainly get a great guy in our dreams, can't we?

B: Why don't we try it? After all, all it takes is one experienced, highly qualified. . .

C: Don't forget! Good looking!

B: *(mildly irritated at being interrupted)* . . . Sandman to get those dreams rolling!

Option 2

A: Mr. Sandman is traditionally considered a folkloric figure.

B: He is known to bring good dreams to little children by sprinkling magical sand onto the eyes while they are asleep.

A: This is said to account for the "sleepy" look in ones eyes *(use the sleepy hand gesture for awakening)* when waking in the morning.

B: Mr. Sandman likes visiting all of us during the night.

A: Yes, a wonderful dream in our imaginations *(pause)* from the sandman.

Mister Sandman

SECTION 7

(This section begins with the choir humming a background for the narration of an appropriately timed section of the song. When the narration is complete, the choir begins the song. Narration is to occur on top of the humming.)

A: Spirituals were used in the quest for freedom. . .

B: and for religious services. . .

C: to educate. . .

A: gossip. . .

B: reprimand. . .

C: signal. . .

A: and for storytelling. *(Valerie DePriest)*

Simple Gifts

SECTION 8

Ain'-a That Good News

SECTION 9

A: During the Victorian era, lovers assembled bouquets for their sweethearts in which each flower or herb meant something.

B: The language of flowers was a not-so-secret code of hidden messages in which parsley meant festivity,

C: Rosemary meant remembrance,

B: Sage stood for esteem and health,

A: And thyme meant activity. *(The Language of Flowers)*

Parsley, Sage, Rosemary, and Thyme

SECTION 10

A: "Without music, life is a journey through a desert." *(Pat Conroy)*

B: "No doctor is capable of healing the intense pain that only music can soothe." *(Stella Rambisi Chiweshe)*

C: "This will be our reply to violence: to make music more intensely, more beautifully, more devotedly than ever before." *(Leonard Bernstein)*

B: Music is our vocabulary; songs are the building blocks of our future.

A: "Music is love, in search of a word." *(Sidney Lanier)*

C: And God said, "Sing!"

I'm Gonna Sing when the Spirit Says Sing

The quotes in this script were taken from the following sources:

Henry David Thoreau

Victor Hugo

Linda Crabtree Powell

Doug Bailey

Steve Rouse

Nathaniel Hawthorne

Valerie DePriest

The Language of Flowers

Paul Burch

Pat Conroy

Stella Rambisi Chiweshe

Leonard Bernstein

Sidney Lanier

The New Testament

WINTER PROGRAMS

Poster by Katherine Szewc

Angels

Title	Composer/Lyricist
Prayer from *Hansel and Gretel*	Engelbert Humperdinck/ Adelheit Wette, trans. C. Bach arr. Wallingford Riegger
alternate selection Evening Prayer from *Hansel and Gretel*	Audrey Snyder
Il est né, le divin enfant (Come and Praise Him the Holy Child)	Gabriel Fauré arr. William Sisson
Lo, How a Rose E'er Blooming	16th c. German, harm. Michael Praetorius trans. Theodore Baker arr. David Shand; John Leavitt
The Christmas Song (Chestnuts Roasting on an Open Fire)	Mel Tormé & Robert Wells arr. Kirby Shaw
Ave Maria	Zoltán Kodály
Carol of the Bells	Mykola Leontovich/ Peter J. Wilhousky arr. Peter J. Wilhousky
Kyrie *(Mass in G Major)*	Franz Schubert/ trans. Patrick M. Liebergen arr. Patrick M. Liebergen
Angels We Have Heard on High	Traditional French carol arr. Mac Huff
Monotone Angel	Don McAfee
Angels, Spread Your Loving Wings	Ruth Elaine Schram/Brian Busch
Jordan's Angels	Rollo Dilworth

Silent Night   Franz Grüber/Joseph Mohr

Night of Silence   Daniel Kantor

This is the only time I've ever had everyone dressed in white—it worked! They were all angels! Audiences remember the funny pieces and in this concert they will remember the "Monotone Angel." Pick someone whose personality fits the character of the angel.

Our tradition with most Christmas programs is to end with "Silent Night" and "Night of Silence." Sing "Silent Night" and "Night of Silence" separately, and then simultaneously with the accompaniment from "Night of Silence." They could also be performed as an encore.

Angels

> *The following program has three narrators. The narrators (A, B, and C) should come from outside the choir. Their voices must blend well together, as there will be some unison speaking. They should practice together prior to their rehearsals with the choir to ensure smooth delivery of the script. They are to stand together on either downstage right or downstage left, close enough to the choir to be an integral part of the performance but also near enough to the audience to provide a connection between them and the choir.*
>
> *The main act curtain is to be closed as the audience enters. When it opens, the lights on stage come up halfway. The choir is to already be in place on the stage, standing quietly. At the same time, a preset spot is to come up on the narrators. Note: The narrators should never speak unless they are in full stage light or under the spot.*

SECTION 1

A: Once upon a time there was, in paradise, a most miserable, thoroughly unhappy, and utterly dejected cherub who was known throughout heaven as

B: The Littlest Angel.

C: The Littlest Angel soon became the despair of all the heavenly host.

A: It was first whispered among the seraphim and cherubim, and then said aloud among the angels and archangels, that he didn't even look like an angel!

B: And they were quite correct.

C: He didn't.

Prayer from *Hansel and Gretel*

SECTION 2

A: His halo was permanently tarnished where he held on to it with one hot, chubby little hand when he ran,

B: and he was always running.

A: And it must be recorded here that his wings were neither useful nor ornamental and whenever he was nervous,

C: which was most of the time,

A, B, C: he bit his wing tips!

A: Now, anyone can easily understand why the Littlest Angel would, sooner or later, have to be disciplined, and although he tried to postpone the dreaded ordeal, he soon found himself reporting to the Understanding Angel and explaining how very difficult it was for a boy who suddenly finds himself transformed into an angel.

Il est né, le divin enfant

SECTION 3

B: Yes, and no matter what the archangels said, he'd only swung once,

A & C: well, twice,

A, B, C: oh, all right, then, he'd swung three times on the golden gates.

A: But that was for something to do!

B: That was the whole trouble. There wasn't anything for a small angel to do.

B: And he was so homesick.

Lo, How a Rose E'er Blooming

SECTION 4

C: Oh, not that paradise wasn't beautiful, but the earth was beautiful, too! Why, there were trees to climb,

B: and brooks to fish,

A: and caves to play at pirate chief,

C: the swimming hole,

B: the sun,

A: and dark,

A, B, C: and the dawn.

The Christmas Song

SECTION 5

B: The Understanding Angel smiled and asked the Littlest Angel what would make him most happy in paradise. The cherub thought for a moment and then whispered in his ear.

A: "There's a box, I left it under my bed back home. If only I could have that."

B: The Understanding Angel nodded.

C: "You shall have it," he promised.

B: And a fleet-winged heavenly messenger was instantly dispatched to bring the box to paradise.

A: And then, everyone wondered at the great change in the Littlest Angel, for among all of the cherubs in God's kingdom, he was happiest.

Ave Maria

SECTION 6

C: It came to pass that Jesus, the Son of God, was to be born to Mary, in Bethlehem, in Judea.

B: And as the glorious tidings spread throughout paradise, all the angels put aside their usual tasks to prepare gifts for the blessed infant.

A: All but the Littlest Angel, who sat down on the topmost step of the golden stairs and anxiously waited for inspiration.

B: What could he give that would be most acceptable to the Son of God?

Carol of the Bells

SECTION 7

C: The time of the miracle was very close at hand when the Littlest Angel at last decided on his gift. On that day of days, with downcast eyes, he humbly placed it before the throne of God.

A: It was only a small, rough, unsightly box, but inside were all those wonderful things that even a child of God would treasure.

Kyrie

Section 8

C: The hand of God moved slowly over all that bright array of shining gifts. . .

B: then paused. . .

A: then dropped. . .

C: then came to rest on the lowly gift of the Littlest Angel!

Angels We Have Heard on High

Section 9

B: The Littlest Angel trembled as the box was opened, and there, before the eyes of God and all the heavenly host, was what he offered to the Christ Child.

A, B, C: And what was his gift to the blessed infant?

Monotone Angel

Section 10

A: Well, there was a butterfly with golden wings, captured one bright summer day on the hills above Jerusalem,

B: and a sky-blue egg from a bird's nest in the olive tree that shaded his mother's kitchen door.

C: Yes, and two white stones, found on a muddy riverbank, where he and his friends had played.

A: At the bottom of the box, a limp, tooth-marked leather strap, once worn as a collar by his mongrel dog, who had died as he had lived, in absolute love

A: and infinite devotion.

Angels, Spread Your Loving Wings

Section 11

C: The Littlest Angel covered his eyes and wept hot, bitter tears.

A: Why had he ever thought that the box was so wonderful?

B: Why had he dreamed that such utterly useless things would be loved by the blessed infant?

C: Then, suddenly, the voice of God, like divine music, rose and swelled throughout paradise.

B: And the voice of God spoke, saying,

A: "Of all the gifts of the angels, I find that this small box pleases me most. Its contents are of the earth and of all people, and these are the things my Son, too, will know and love and cherish."

Jordan's Angels

SECTION 12

C: There was a breathless pause, and then the rough, unsightly box of the Littlest Angel began to glow with a bright, unearthly light,

B: then the light became a lustrous flame

A: and the flame became a radiant brilliance that blinded the eyes of all the angels!

B: None but the Littlest Angel saw it rise from its place before the throne of God.

C: And he,

B: and only he,

A: watched it arch away from heaven and shed its clear, white, beckoning light over a stable where a child was born.

A: There it shone on the night of miracles,

B: and its light was reflected down the centuries deep in the heart of all humankind

C: and we would call it forever,

A, B, C: the shining star of Bethlehem.

Silent Night and Night of Silence

Sing "Silent Night" and "Night of Silence" separately, and then simultaneously with the accompaniment from "Night of Silence."

TRINITY HIGH SCHOOL
FINE ARTS DEPARTMENT PRESENTS

Be Joyful!

DECEMBER 18, 2013

Choral Concert 7:00 PM

Gallery Opens 6:30 PM

7574 W Division St., River Forest, IL

Poster by Maddie McPhillips

Be Joyful!

Title	Composer/Lyricist
It's the Most Wonderful Time of the Year	Eddie Pola & George Wyle arr. Alan Billingsley
Hot Chocolate	Glen Ballard & Alan Silvestri arr. Roger Emerson
Merrily Sing Noel!	Linda Spevacek
My Favorite Things *The Sound of Music*	Richard Rogers/Oscar Hammerstein II arr. Mac Huff
Believe *The Polar Express*	Glen Ballard & Alan Billingsley arr. Mark Hayes
Patapan	Bernard de La Monnoye/ Burgundian carol trans. Sandra Peter
Joy to the World *(handchimes)*	George Frideric Handel & Lowell Mason/ Isaac Watts
Count Your Blessings Instead of Sheep	Irving Berlin arr. Cristi Cary Miller
Sing a Joyful Song *out of print*	Patsy Ford Simms
alternate selection Alleluia! I Will Sing	David Waggoner
Hail Holy Queen *Sister Act*	Traditional/adapt. Roger Emerson arr. Marc Shaiman
alternate selection Linus and Lucy	Vince Guaraldi arr. Philip Kern
We Three Kings	John Henry Hopkins, Jr. arr. Russell Robinson
Ode to Joy *(handchimes)*	Ludwig van Beethoven
Joyfully Sing!	Linda Spevacek
Breath of Heaven (Mary's Song)	Amy Grant & Chris Eaton arr. Roger Emerson
What Strangers Are These?	Old Scottish carol arr. Peter Stone

The Holly and the Ivy	Old English carol
out of print	arr. Peter Ston
alternate arrangement	arr. Ron Jeffers
Carol of the Bells	Mykola Wilhousky/
	Peter J. Wilhousky
	arr. Peter J. Wilhousky
Good King Kong Looked Out	Peter Schickele (as P. D. Q. Bach)
Sing for Joy!	George F. Handel
Judas Maccabaeus	arr. Linda Spevacek

Hearing kazoos put a smile on everyone's face. Peter Schickele must have had that in mind when he altered the familiar carol lyrics to create "Good King Kong Looked Out."

Handchimes create a joyful sound with a simple melody, especially on Beethoven's "Ode to Joy" or a version of "Joy to the World." We used the harmonized versions from a traditional hymnal for all handchime pieces.

A link to a YouTube video of a program excerpt is available at www.giamusic.com/ccc.

Be Joyful!

Opening

> *For pre-house opening, play holiday music to set a joyful mood. When the house lights go down the last piece the audience should be hearing is "It's the Most Wonderful Time of the Year." At the end of the music, house lights have dimmed and sleigh bells are heard as the curtain opens. Each singer should be wearing two from the following list: 1) a hat (not covering ears), 2) a scarf, and 3) gloves or mittens. Lots of color is recommended. The choir listens for an instrumental cue to begin singing. Singers should be positioned off the risers and there should be choreography. You may use one continuous narrator or several narrators for this program.*

Section 1

It's the Most Wonderful Time of the Year

Section 2

Hello, friends. I've traveled here from a place that you know well: it's called *joy*. And tonight I'm here to remind you—through sights and sounds—where joy is, what joy is, and how joy feels. We don't have to go to joy. It comes to us in an instant, through surprising channels. Joy can slip in silently with the falling of a sparkling midnight snow; joy can bubble up at the sound of a child's laughter; joy can fly in our window with an invigorating breeze. And as you'll hear right now, joy can be found in something as simple as a cup of hot chocolate!

Hot Chocolate

Section 3

How do you find your way to joy? Do you contemplate the things you love? Do certain images make you smile, like raindrops on roses and whiskers on kittens? Then you'll feel happy contemplating your favorite things. But joy may be found in much deeper things: in your very soul, where your beliefs are rooted. What do you believe in? Do you believe in love? In life? Let yourself travel inward, to the things you love, and the things you live for.

Favorite Things

Believe

Section 4

Option 1

Do you hear that? Listen! In the dark night, a blanket of stars illuminates the shepherds and their flocks; they are filled with wonder, and they play their crude instruments in celebration of the birth of a child. Pat-pat, bum-bum, pat-a-pan. In this old carol, which originated in a region of France called Burgundy, we hear joy in the sound of a drum—in the rhythmic thrumming that is meant to echo the beating of our hearts, which cry out to the new King! What song would you play, under the light of those stars, knowing that the world would never be the same? What rhythm would express your inexpressible joy?

Option 2

Do you hear that? Listen. In the dark night, there can be heard the sound of a drum, signaling a joyful heart. It starts out slowly, softly, but then reaches a crescendo, a steady thrumming as beautiful as a heartbeat. Pat-pat, bum-bum, pat-a-pan. Enjoy this the old Burgundian carol, "Patapan," and feel the joy of the ancient music!

Patapan

transition music

Handchimes: Joy to the World

SECTION 5

Joy can come quietly. It's not only about counting our favorite things—it's about counting our blessings. When we do, we find that they outnumber our cares, and that for every silver snowflake that falls, we can name a blessing that has been bestowed on us. Bing Crosby sang to Rosemary Clooney about counting blessings in the classic film *White Christmas*.

Count Your Blessings

SECTION 6

Option 1

One person knew joy better than anyone else on earth. One woman, who traveled far at great personal sacrifice, through dark nights and darker fears, only to be told there was no room for her in the inn where she hoped to have her child. And yet, cast out, dismissed, in pain, she stayed focused on the message of her God and the birth of her son. And in the face of that child, she saw the light that believers today experience only through the Gospel. She saw the face of love and named him Jesus, and her joy was complete. We cannot think of Christmas joy without imagining the life of Mary, the mother of God, and the promise of the child that she held against her heart.

Option 2

In the movie *Sister Act*, Whoopie Goldberg's character, who is not a nun but a nightclub singer, manages to transform a staid choir of sisters into a joyful group of singers. She takes their slow hymn and turns it into a rhythmic, fun celebration of love. Here is their new song: "Hail Holy Queen."

Hail Holy Queen

alternate selection and narration

> One of the most beautiful summations of the meaning of Christmas was spoken by a little boy named Linus in Charlie Brown's Christmas special, which first aired in 1965. Linus understood the value of joy—its simplicity, its availability, its eternal presence. He shared it with his friends in his sweet recitation of a Biblical verse, and in the sharing of his beloved blanket, which transformed a "loser" tree into something that brought great light and happiness. Linus understood joy, and it is irrepressibly expressed in Vince Guaraldi's "Linus and Lucy."

Linus and Lucy

We Three Kings

transition music

HANDCHIMES: Ode to Joy

SECTION 7

Option 1

Joy can be elusive, but we search for it. Long ago, three kings came together to follow a tantalizing star—a star whose light promised joy—and through many dark nights the kings pursued the light in the darkness that meant the birth of a child. That child, they knew, would bring joy to all the world. With joy, we celebrate those kings, who heralded the birth of Christ.

Option 2

Beautiful sounds are signals of joy. In holiday music, we let music and praise fill the air, and "hear how the sounds rejoice everywhere." Let the music fill your heart at this special time of year, and joyfully sing.

Joyfully Sing

SECTION 8

Option 1

Sometimes, in focusing on the child who was meant to save the world, we forget about his mother—Mary, meek and mild; Mary, sweet and unassuming. Yet Mary had the strength to accept God within herself, and to stand up to those who would question her. She rode, heavy with child, not knowing where she would give birth to him. For Mary, there were many questions in the dark night, but her faith was its own light, and her joy was guaranteed. She named him Jesus.

Option 2

Beautiful music is like the anticipation of heaven, just as a mother, awaiting birth, anticipates the joyous meeting with her child—a sort of heaven on earth that brings peace and eternal love. Music and heaven—there is a link between them that all musicians know. Experience it in the song "Breath of Heaven."

Breath of Heaven

What Strangers Are These?

SECTION 9

Joy can be found in tradition. We all share traditions that bring us happiness, from decorating with ivy to decorating the tree. In these traditional carols, we celebrate the joy brought by the sight of the bright, festive red holly berries, lush green ivy leaves, and by the sound of bells. For what are holidays without bells?

The Holly and the Ivy

Carol of the Bells

SECTION 10

Joy is often expressed in laughter. When Peter Schickele created his fictional musical character, P. D. Q. Bach, he attributed many compositions to this "only forgotten son" of the Bach family. One of those tunes is a Christmas carol that is vaguely reminiscent of "Good King Wenceslas" and other English tunes. P. D. Q. Bach's version, though, is called "Good King Kong Looked Out," and the joy of this piece is in its delightful absurdity!

Good King Kong Looked Out

SECTION 11

What is joy? Joy is jubilation, triumph, exultation. Joy is the velvet skin of a baby's cheek or the gentle nuzzle of a beloved pet's nose. Joy is a family member returning from far away; joy is the sound of music. Joy is a candle that illuminates the darkness; joy is the rain that patters against the window and the silent snow that falls in the night. Joy is in unexpected laughter and happy tears. Joy is in every compliment and kind thought. Joy is in this room, passing from one person to the next, and from our music into your hearts.

Keep joy with you, but don't be afraid to give it away. Joy multiplies itself. May joy leave with you tonight and be with you until we meet on another evening . . .

Sing for Joy

Closing

At the beginning of the evening, I told you that joy is a place, and now you have been there. You do not need a map to joy; as you found it tonight, so you will find it again—or it will find you!

CHOIR and audience: a holiday carol

TRINITY HIGH SCHOOL
Fine Arts Department
Presents

Colors of Christmas

7574 W Division St, River Forest, IL

December 19th
2012

6:30 pm
Gallery Opens

7:00 pm
Choral Concert

Poster by Nicole Levar

Colors of Christmas

Title	Composer/Lyricist
Christmas Time is Here	Lee Mendelson & Vince Guaraldi arr. Teena Chinn
Cool Yule	Steve Allen arr. Kirby Shaw
Beacon Hill Carol	Irish Air arr. Stephen Hatfield
Winter Wonderland	Felix Benard/Dick Smith arr. Leo Arnaud
The Christmas Song	Mel Tormé & Robert Wells arr. Kirby Shaw
What Child Is This?	"Greensleeves" melody
Carol of the Bells	Mykola Leontovich/ Peter J. Wilhousky arr. Peter J. Wilhousky
Silver Bells *out of print*	Jay Livingston & Ray Evans arr. George Terry
Poor Mary *out of print*	Katherine K. Davis/John Cowley
alternate selection Child of God	Spiritual Emily Crocker
Colors of Winter	Amy F. Bernon
Ave Maria (Angelus Domini)	Franz Biebl/anon.
White Christmas	Irving Berlin arr. Roy Ringwald
Blue Christmas	Billy Hayes & Jay Johnson arr. Mac Huff
Jingle Bells Hallelujah	James L. Pierpont & George Frideric Handel arr. Jonathan Miller

Silent Night　　　　　　　　　　Franz Grüber/Joseph Mohr

Night of Silence　　　　　　　　Daniel Kantor

> *If it's winter, there should be snow. Buy some fake snow, readily available at stores during the holidays, for the closing of your program. If there is a catwalk, a small stage crew can gently drop the snow from over head. It should be practiced and look realistic. Another option is to have singers throw snow up in the air at the end. It's not going to melt so it can be held in their hands and passed out during the narration interval. Any method you use should be practiced. You're bound to get some "ahs" of surprise and enjoyment. For our winter programs, it has become a tradition.*
>
> *We used the harmonized version of "What Child Is This?" from a traditional hymnal for handchimes to play.*
>
> *You may decide to close the program with "Jingle Bells Hallelujah." It should be switched in the order with "Blue Christmas" if it is the last selection.*
>
> *Our tradition with most Christmas programs is to end with "Silent Night" and "Night of Silence." Sing "Silent Night" and "Night of Silence" separately, and then simultaneously with the accompaniment from "Night of Silence." They could also be performed as an encore.*
>
> *A link to a YouTube video of a program excerpt is available at www.giamusic.com/ccc.*

Colors of Christmas

> *This program requires one narrator. The focus of this program is that of memories, particularly those memories that are centered on Christmas and which are stirred up by the colors associated with that holiday. We hope that the imagination of the audience members will connect with what is being presented on stage, and that all will relate emotionally to both the words that are being spoken and the songs that are being sung.*

Opening

Ah, Christmas! It's the most wonderful time of the year. There are the beautiful Christmas songs, the decorated trees, the excitement of opening presents, and the shared sacred solemnity of family and friends gathered together to celebrate the birth of the Christ Child. However, what means most to so many of us are the deeply treasured memories of Christmases past. Inspired by a snatch of song, the scent of baking permeating the air with cinnamon and cloves, or the sight of a cheerfully wrapped package just begging to be opened, our Christmas memories can surface at any time or in any place. More than anything else, memories of the holidays can be stirred by the colors of Christmas.

Section 1

To me, Christmas always meant going to my grandparents' house. My parents, my little sister Annie, and I would leave our city apartment early morning on Christmas Eve. As we drove first down city streets and eventually onto snow-packed country roads, anticipation would build until we could hardly stand it. Then, suddenly, there it was—a pretty red brick house with dark green shutters and evergreen bushes festooned with heavy caps of drooping white snow. As we'd jump out of the car, the front door would open and the golden glow of firelight would spill out onto the snow. "Welcome, darlings!" cried Grandpa and Grandma. "Come on in! Christmas time is here!"

Christmas Time Is Here

SECTION 2

Grandpa already had the tree up, standing tall and proud in the corner of the living room, waiting for Annie and me to decorate it. One of our favorite boxes of ornaments was a collection of small musical instruments. Rendered in exquisite detail, the tiny instruments glowed in silver, brass, and gold. The trumpets and saxophones looked ready to play, and we could almost hear the clarinet wailing out a jazz tune. The trumpet and the saxophone would join in, adding richer textures to the high sweet sound of the clarinet. Annie and I pretended to play the little ornaments, and—dancing around the living room—we insisted we were ushering in a totally "Cool Yule."

Cool Yule

SECTION 3

Grandma's favorite Christmas ornament was a small green felt shamrock. Its four leaves and stem were edged with clumsy red silk stitches, and in the center were the slightly tipsy initials, "A. K. S." standing for my great-great-grandmother's name. The thread had once been shiny and bright, but age had faded it to a dull maroon. "This ornament was made by my great-grandmother," Grandma explained. "She was six years old and just learning how to sew. Her family was immigrating to America, and she wanted to bring something with her to remind her of her beloved Ireland, so she chose to make this little shamrock. These are her initials. They stand for 'Annie Kathleen Sinclair.' You were named after her, Annie, and someday it will be you who hangs your great-great-grandmother's ornament on your own family Christmas tree." Grandma would smile at my little sister and then, holding Annie's hand in hers, together they would hang the green felt shamrock in a place of honor on the Christmas tree.

Beacon Hill

SECTION 4
Winter Wonderland

SECTION 5

One of Grandpa's prized possessions was his old stereo record player, and he was equally proud of his record collection, which took up an entire shelf of the bookcase. He played his records often, and told us he considered them old friends. Of course I tried to interest him in my little cassette player, but he said he did not care for it—his fingers were too big for its tiny buttons and besides, it was his opinion that his old 33-and-1/3 records gave him the best tone quality possible. He'd carefully wipe off one of his favorite records, slide it onto the machine, gently push the play lever, and watch the needle swing over and drop into place. Then Grandma would hand me the old popcorn popper that she had just filled with bright yellow kernels of corn, and say, "Here, honey, shake this over the flames in the fireplace." I'd sit as close to the fire as possible, enjoying its orange glow and fiery red embers as Grandpa's Christmas song played softly in the background. The song was the perfect choice for Christmas, a fire, and a little girl shaking a popcorn popper over the flames. Grandpa always called the song by its proper title, "The Christmas Song," but Annie and I just called it "Chestnuts Roasting on an Open Fire."

The Christmas Song

SECTION 6

One of the dominant Christmas colors is green—the rich glossy green of holly leaves, the green of the evergreens, the green of the candles decorating Grandpa and Grandma's dining room table. Green is also in the name of one the oldest of our Christmas melodies: "Greensleeves." "What Child Is This?" the modern Christmas version asks, and the answer comes, "I think I know." We know, too, as we share the warmth of the fire and the love of our family.

HANDCHIMES: What Child Is This?

SECTION 7

How I loved cooking with Grandma! My favorite kitchen task was to help her bake Christmas cookies. Decked out in one of her oversized aprons, I would gently press a bell-shaped cookie cutter into the chilled rolled-out dough. Then, oh joy of joys! It was my job to decorate the cookies by carefully pouring on tiny silver balls of candy, being sure to fill in all the empty spaces until each cookie was a solid bell of silver. Grandma would then bake the cookies in a 350-degree oven for 10 minutes. We would fill a plate with the silver bell cookies and use them to decorate the Christmas buffet. We loved those delicious cookies, those "sweet silver bells."

Carol of the Bells

SECTION 8

Silver bells also decorated the Christmas tree. Grandma's mother, my great-grandma, was the one who had originally collected the bells; she had one bell for each of her eight children. Annie and I polished the tarnish off the beautiful bells by gently rubbing each one with a buffing cloth until the silver glowed. Then we hung the bells on the tree, where they glittered back at us from the dark green branches.

Silver Bells

SECTION 9

Option 1

There was a star on our Christmas tree, a bright gold star edged with a golden fringe. Because it had to be at the very tippy-top, Grandpa always set it in place immediately after putting up the tree. Balancing carefully on his ladder, Grandpa would use his penknife to shave off all the needles from the uppermost shaft of the tree, and then, ever so carefully, he would clip the star to the branch. I remember how, even when all of the lights had been turned off, the star would still sparkle. A golden star hovered over a stable in Bethlehem, too, lighting the way for the three kings as they journeyed to Mary and the Christ Child. Poor Mary had nothing but a cow's manger in which to lay her newborn babe, but the lowly stable shimmered in the golden glow of a star sent straight from heaven above.

Poor Mary

Option 2

Spirituals have long played an important part of black America's choral history. Stories were passed down through song and shared in each generation. It's easy to imagine this rocking lullaby being sung to a young child slowly falling to sleep. Every mother has a memory of their sleeping—or soon to be asleep—child. I remember my mother singing me to sleep. . .

Child of God

Section 10

While Annie and I were busy decorating the tree, Grandpa was testing and hanging the tree lights. Every bulb had to be checked to see if it was screwed in tightly enough and replaced if it were burned out. No bulbs of the same color could ever be next to each other, so the entire procedure took Grandpa some time to complete. It was all worth it, though, for when the tree lights were finally hung and plugged in, the Christmas tree looked magical! Annie and I would turn out all the other lights so we could just sit and admire the Christmas lights and their red, blue, green, and yellow glow.

Colors of Winter

SECTION 11

Option 1

Standing on the fireplace mantle and surrounded by evergreen branches and white votive candles was a statue of the Virgin Mary. Her hair was hidden beneath a blue veil, over which floated a halo of tiny golden stars. Her cheeks were a delicate pink and her lips a soft rose. Her hands were clasped in front of her white gown as though in prayer. It was my absolutely favorite statue of the Virgin because her face was so tender, her eyes so full of love. When I stood in front of that beautiful statue, I felt as though the Virgin Mary was seeing me, smiling at me, and I was humbled by her love.

Option 2

In Bavaria, Germany, community singing has been a long tradition. In 1964, Franz Biebl was asked to compose an Ave Maria commissioned by the local firehouse. Imagine a brigade of singing fireman performing an ancient liturgical text, and the mountains capped with white in the distance behind a picturesque town.

Ave Maria

SECTION 12

Going to sleep on Christmas Eve was so difficult. Annie and I would snuggle together in our mother's old bed, whispering about the next day, hoping for some special gift, and anticipating the delicious traditional Christmas brunch Grandma was so famous for. Most of all we would hope for a fresh coating of snow to blanket the back yard, rendering it perfect for sledding. After all of the presents had been unwrapped, Annie and I would don our snowsuits and boots and, dragging our sleds behind us, trudge into the back yard where we would spend hours swooping down the snowy hill. Ah, snow—fresh white snow. We would finally fall asleep dreaming of a white Christmas.

White Christmas

SECTION 13

Option 1

We would awaken on Christmas morning to sleigh bells as Grandpa roamed the upstairs hall, shaking a strip of sleigh bells and announcing to all, "Wake up! The Christ Child has been born! It's Christmas morning and time to celebrate his birth! Wake up! Wake up!" And the bells would jingle outside our door until we jumped out of bed and let him in for a morning kiss. Ah! The happy ringing of jingle bells.

Option 2

I remember hearing bells from the famous reindeer right outside our door. Excitedly I rushed to the window and declared I had seen them in the sky. Everyone smiled. Years later I found out that I had heard bells, but they weren't on the reindeer! My dad, who happened to be outside, was carrying a strip of sleigh bells. Listen carefully, because these jingle bells have a way of switching around, too.

Jingle Bells Hallelujah

SECTION 14

One of Grandpa's favorite Christmas records was Elvis Presley singing holiday songs. He'd play that record, along with some of his other favorites, on Christmas morning. Grandma was not too sure she approved of Elvis. *She* claimed he did some suspicious shenanigans while he was performing, but Grandpa always reassured her by saying that Elvis behaved himself when singing Christmas tunes. "The boy has a good voice," he'd say, "and it's only when he's singing some nonsense about hound dogs or jailhouses that he loses control of himself. When he's singing hymns or Christmas music, why he's as good as it gets." And so along with Bing Crosby and Lawrence Welk, we'd have Elvis on Christmas morning. One of his songs made me sad, however. It was the one where he sang about a lost love. The holidays just weren't the same without her, he'd sing, and so he was having a blue, blue Christmas.

Blue Christmas

Closing

SECTION 15

Option 1

The vibrant colors of Christmas were all around us: the red of the holly berries, the green of our Christmas tree, and the white of the snow. The silver Christmas bells and the gold tree ornaments shimmered before our eyes. To this day, the colors of Christmas remind us of the beauty of the holiday, the glory of the Christmas story, and the warmth of families gathered together in celebration. Most of all, the colors of Christmas remind us of love, unconditional love, pure and freely given. It is the love of humble shepherds searching for a newborn King, the love of a mother for her sweet little babe, the love of our Father who gave us his only-begotten son. The colors of Christmas—the reds, greens, blues, golds, and silvers—are all the colors of love.

Option 2

We see all the vibrant colors of holidays all around us: red of the holly berries, green from evergreen trees, white of the snow, shimmering lights, and sparkles of silver and gold. All of these colors are a part of everyone's Christmas memories. When we reflect, they remind us of what is really important in life—to love and be loved.

Encore

> CHOIR and audience: **Silent Night** and **Night of Silence**, *or another familiar carol. Sing "Silent Night" and "Night of Silence" separately, and then simultaneously with the accompaniment from "Night of Silence."*

Poster by Martha Chlipala

Food, Fun, and Festivities!

Title	Composer/Lyricist
Jingle Bells	James Pierpont/adapt. Mark Hayes arr. Jack Gold & Marty Paich
I'll Give My Love an Apple	English folk song arr. Eleanor Daley
My Favorite Things *The Sound of Music*	Richard Rogers/Oscar Hammerstein II arr. Mac Huff
Velvet Shoes	Randall Thompson/Elinor Wylie arr. David A. Seitz
Food, Glorious Food *Oliver*	Lionel Bart arr. Aden G. Lewis
Dance of the Sugar Plum Fairy	Pyotr Ilyich Tchaikovsky arr. Jeff Funk
Parsley, Sage, Rosemary, and Thyme	Old English song arr. John Coates, Jr.
Baby, It's Cold Outside	Frank Loesser arr. Kirby Shaw
Winter Carnival	Danish folk dance/ Katharine Whitmore, alt. arr. Linda Spevacek
The Snow	Edward Elgar/C. Alice Elgar
Hot Chocolate	Glen Ballard & Alan Silvestri arr. Roger Emerson
Sleigh Ride	LeRoy Anderson/Mitchell Parish arr. Andy Beck

This program should naturally be followed with a food reception. Determine what type of food you would like to offer, such as cookies, candy, soup, sandwiches, cider, or hot chocolate. Perhaps this could be used as a choir fundraiser. It is a good idea for your audience and singers to have an opportunity to meet and visit after the program. A reception can continue the "food, fun, and festivities."

Food, Fun, and Festivities!

> *There should be preset music as the audience enters. A recommended selection is "Winter" from Vivaldi's* Four Seasons. *Avoid vocal music with lyrics.*
>
> *Two narrators should be selected who are not members of the choir. They should be good readers and able to speak expressively. They will not start until after the opening song.*
>
> *The lights come down as we hear sleigh bells ringing, and the curtain opens to choir members spread around the performance area. Each singer should wear two of these: a colorful scarf, gloves, or a hat (with nothing over their ears) over black concert attire. The opening should have some choreography created by the director, a choreographer, or a student with some dance background. It is important to start with energy, smiles, and good lighting on the singers' faces.*

Opening

Jingle Bells

> *Narrators begin walking out near the end of the piece to enjoy the piece of music. They are also dressed for winter and can change their accessories during the program. They could both be girls or a boy/girl combination. Good smiles and an easy laugh are particularly important for this theme.*

Section 1

Narrator A: That was a great song. Nothing captures the feeling of winter like the jingling of bells.

Narrator B: That's true—bells get you in the spirit of the season, a time when people draw close together in the cold air, and their hearts grow warmer because of it.

A: Sometimes those hearts can fall in love. *(pause)* Listen to this traditional folk tune "I'll Give My Love an Apple" and let it fill your heart with the gentle warmth of the season.

FOOD, FUN, AND FESTIVITIES!

I'll Give My Love an Apple

SECTION 2

A: Ah, I love that song. What beautiful images—it reminds me of so many of my favorite things.

B: Really, what are some of your other favorite things?

A: I love all kinds of things about this season. The snowflakes, the soft footsteps on an early morning snowfall, the hot chocolate with marshmallows. . .

B: How about crisp apple strudels, bright copper kettles, and warm woolen mittens?

A: I see where this is going! We're going to listen to "My Favorite Things," the Rodgers and Hammerstein classic from *The Sound of Music!*

B: Yes, we are. And let it inspire you to think of your own favorite things, too.

My Favorite Things

SECTION 3

A: In the winter, I have to change my entire wardrobe. I need a warm coat, gloves, boots, hat, and scarves, and I'm still sometimes cold.

B: Well, have you ever walked in the snow with velvet shoes?

Velvet Shoes

SECTION 4

A: That was such a beautiful image of winter. Did you ever notice that besides being cold you also feel hungrier during this season? It must take all our body energy to keep warm but regardless of the reason, I love to eat. *(smile)*

B: Me, too. And glorious food was always on the mind of the hungry orphans in *Oliver!*

Food, Glorious Food

SECTION 5

A: There are so many things to do during winter. I like dancing.

B: Really, what kind of dancing do you do?

A: Well, I've tried lots of different styles, like tap, modern, hip-hop, ballet...

B: Ballet? You must know the famous *Nutcracker* suite ballet! How could you draw close to the many festivities of winter without hearing the classical music of Tchaikovsky? Let's listen to a vocal version now. This is the beautiful Dance of the Sugar Plum Fairy who rules the Land of Sweets in the kingdom of Clara's prince. (*to the other narrator*) Do you remember?

A: Yes, and the Land of Sweets sounds very appealing!

Dance of the Sugar Plum Fairy

SECTION 6

A: Oh, that was so much fun to hear the voices sounding like instruments! Did you like it?

B: Yes, but it put me in the mood for food! Something about daydreaming my way into the land of sweets...

A: Well then, why don't we daydream our way into Scarborough Fair and inhale all the fragrant herbs?

B: *(inhaling deeply)* You mean parsley, sage, rosemary, and thyme?

A: Yes! And that famous refrain. There are many versions of this English folk ballad which date all the way back to the 18th century, but the most famous version was sung by Simon and Garfunkel in the 1960s, and that tends to be the one we think of today. Let's listen to our own choral version as we recall those fragrant herbs known to us all.

Parsley, Sage, Rosemary, and Thyme

Section 7

B. That was fun! But it made me even hungrier, somehow!

A: Food is such an integral part of the winter season! Our appetites waken as we fight off the cold. We like to cuddle together and share food and wine, and they warm us, body and soul.

B: Hey, that reminds me of the next song, where a man tries to convince a girl not to go out into the cold weather, but to stay in his warm arms, drinking wine, eating a meal—and kissing him!

A: Oh yes–such a romantic classic. Hey Baby, It's Cold Outside!

Baby, It's Cold Outside

Section 8

B: Brrr. . . That song makes me think it's better to stay out of the snow.

A: But sometimes the best part of winter is going out in the snow and discovering the beautiful crystalline world that has been created! One needs to have fun in the snow.

B: Perhaps that's best represented by our next song, a traditional Danish carol about enjoying the cold months with festivals and song, with some added stomps and claps, too. It's called "Winter Carnival."

Winter Carnival

Section 9

A: Snow has such a magical effect, particularly the first time it's covering the ground.

B: True, we tend to forget their beauty until we see the first glittering snowflakes arrive.

A: "They show their beauty yet melt away

   they make a lovely, snowy day."

B: Well, I think I prefer the lyrics by Alice Elgar. Alice was married to Edward Elgar, who was an English composer who lived from 1857 to 1934. He published "The Snow" in 1895. Listen now.

The Snow

SECTION 10

B: Winter

A: Snow

B: Bells

B: Mittens

A: Hot soups

B: Delicious chili

A: Warm sandwiches

B: Piping tea

A: Cold

B: Hot *(starting to think ahead)*

B: Whipped cream. . . *(reaching the same conclusion)*

A & B together: *(look at each other and smile)* Hhhot Chocolate!

Hot Chocolate

Closing

SECTION 11

A: Oh, that was great. I could almost taste the hot chocolate.

B: But not quite, huh? So I suppose you still want to find something to eat?

A: Yes, let's go get our own hot chocolate. Now let's take one last ride through our winter daydream, in our own beautiful sleigh, with a fuzzy blanket over us, and a beautiful white horse at the end of our reins. We'll watch his hooves go clip, clop, clip as he trots through the

FOOD, FUN, AND FESTIVITIES!

snowy landscape, and lose ourselves in a dream of winter beauty.

B: *(sighing)* That sounds perfect. *(turning to the audience)* And you're all invited to come join us on our beautiful, "fun" sleigh ride!

A & B (together): Let's go!!

Sleigh bells immediately start again like the opening.

Sleigh Ride

See stage directions on page 100 for snow at closing.

Trinity High School Fine Arts Show
December 16, 2009

"A Light in the Night"

Bianca Medina, '10

6:30 Gallery Opening
& Instrumental Ensemble
On view~ our student artists' recent work

7:00 Choral Concert
Bel Coro, Chamber Choir, Le Ragazze
and guests~ St Patrick's Men's Choir

Reception immediately following the concert

Admission: FREE!

Trinity High School auditorium

Poster by Bianca Medina

A Light in the Night

Title	Composer/Lyricist
Jesu, Joy of Man's Desiring	Johann Sebastian Bach arr. Wallingford Riegger
Sleigh Ride	LeRoy Anderson/Mitchell Parish arr. Andy Beck
White Christmas	Irving Berlin/LeRoy Anderson arr. Roy Ringwald
Go, Tell It on the Mountain	Traditional spiritual arr. Patsy Simms
Merry Christmas, Darling	Frank Pooler & Richard Carpenter arr. Mac Huff
Two Wassails	Traditional British carols Wassail Song & Gloucestershire Wassail
out of print	arr. Tom Johnson
alternate selection Wassail	Traditional arr. Jerry Rubino
What Child Is This?	Traditional English melody/ William Chatterton Dix
Ubi Caritas	Ola Gjeilo
Carol of the Bells	Mykola Leontovich/ Peter J. Wilhousky arr. Peter J. Wilhousky
Dance of the Sugar Plum Fairy *The Nutcracker*	Pyotr Ilyich Tchaikovsky arr. Jeff Funk
Angels Watchin' Over Me	Spiritual arr. Patsy Ford Simms
Silent Night	Franz Grüber/Joseph Mohr
Night of Silence	Daniel Kantor

Even if you have minimal lighting effects they can enhance your performance. Flashlight choreography works with the "Dance of the Sugar Plum Fairy." The more lights you can use in your group, the better. Leave the singing to a select group so the others can concentrate on what they are doing with that on/off switch. It needs to be rehearsed in the dark to see how it really looks. This was a big hit.

A Light in the Night can also close with "Angels Watchin' Over Me." "Silent Night" and "Night of Silence" may be omitted, sung separately, or sung simultaneously with the accompaniment from "Night of Silence." This may also be an encore.

Here is a poem by Rhonda Rickard that you might want to include in the printed program:

There is light in the morning,

There is light at the end of the tunnel,

There is light as you slip the switch,

But, the light that shines the brightest,

Is the light that shines from within.

A Light in the Night

> *The following program calls for the use of one narrator. Note: The sources of the quotes used in this program are not to be read aloud by the narrator, but instead included in the program in a list at the end.*

Opening

> *Curtain warmers up on main act curtain. Choir should be in place behind main act for first song. Open main curtain slowly and evenly while bringing up stage lights to halfway. Spot up on narrator. When narrator has completed first remarks, spot off and stage lights up.*

SECTION 1

Throughout history, the night sky has inspired writers of poetry, literature, and song, infusing people around the world with a sense of wonder and spirituality.

Jesu, Joy of Man's Desiring

SECTION 2

"Sirius, the brightest star in the heavens . . . my grandfather would say we're part of something incredibly wonderful—more marvelous than we imagine. My grandfather would say we ought to go out and look at it once in a while so we don't lose our place in it." *(Robert Fulgham)*

Sleigh Ride

SECTION 3

There is only one color for me when I think of a winter wonderland, and that is the color white. What else could it be? We all hope for the peace and beauty of a winter wonderland, and this is especially so on Christmas morning. The untouched white blanket of snow, the heavy-laden evergreens, their fragile boughs bowed under mounds of white crystals, and the peace and stillness that permeates the atmosphere that surrounds us. All this is what we dream of when we hear the beautiful melody of the song "White Christmas."

White Christmas

Section 4

"The heavens declare the glory of God, and the firmament showeth his handiwork." *(Psalm 19:1)*

Go Tell It on the Mountain

Section 5

"Doubt thou the stars are fire;

Doubt that the sun doth move;

Doubt the truth to be a liar;

But never doubt I love." (William Shakespeare, *Hamlet*, Act II, sc ii)

Merry Christmas Darling

Section 6

"It is he who maketh the stars (as beacons) for you, that ye may guide yourselves, with their help, through the dark spaces of land and seas..." *(The Holy Qur'an 006:097 An'am)*

Two Wassails (Wassail Song & Gloucestershire Wassail)

alternative selection

Wassail

SECTION 7

Option 1

"Now after Jesus was born in Bethlehem of Judea in the days of Herod the king, behold, wise men from the East came to Jerusalem, saying, 'Where is He who has been born King of the Jews? For we have seen His star in the East and have come to worship Him.'" *(Matthew 2:1-2)*

Option 2

There are many myths that cloud the tune's origins in mystery. It is a lamenting lovers hymn from some gentleman to his "Lady Greensleeves." Legend has it that King Henry VIII wrote it for Anne Boleyn during their courtship around 1530, but there is no substantial evident to back this up. The melody is thought to have originated in the late 1500s. After the American Civil War, William Chatterton Dix used the melody to write the popular carol, "What Child is This?"

What Child Is This?

SECTION 8

Option 1

"Herod, when he had secretly called the wise men, determined from them what time the star appeared. And he sent them to Bethlehem and said 'Go and search carefully for the young child, and when you have found Him, bring back word to me, that I may come and worship Him also.' When they heard the king, they departed; and behold, the star which they had seen in the East went before them, till it came and stood over where the young Child was." *(Matthew 2:7)*

Option 2

"Love is not patronizing and charity isn't about pity, it is about love. Charity and love are the same—with charity you give love, so don't just give money but reach out your hand instead." *(Mother Teresa)*

Ubi Caritas

Section 9

"I have loved the stars too fondly to be fearful of the night."
(*Sarah Williams*)

> *Consider using one of the handchimes to give the first pitch for "Carol of the Bells" to the choir as they rearrange their position. This selection is effective sung in small mixed ensembles.*

Carol of the Bells

Section 10

"The stars hang bright above, silent, as if they watched the sleeping earth." *(Sarah Williams)*

Dance of the Sugar Plum Fairy

Section 11

"Perhaps they are not stars, but rather openings in Heaven where the love of our lost ones pours through and shines down upon us to let us know they are happy." *(inspired by an Eskimo legend)*

Angels Watchin' over Me

Section 12

"Every great dream begins with a dreamer. Always remember, you have within you the strength, the patience, and the passion to reach for the stars to change the world." *(Harriet Tubman)*

Optional Choir Closing:

> Choir and audience: **Silent Night** and **Night of Silence**, *or another familiar carol. Sing "Silent Night" and "Night of Silence" separately, and then simultaneously with the accompaniment from "Night of Silence."*

Closing

SECTION 13

"Silently, one by one, in the infinite meadows of the heavens, blossomed the lovely stars, the forget-me-nots of the angels."

(Henry Wadsworth Longfellow, Evangeline, *1847)*

The quotes used in this program are from these sources and authors:

Robert Fulgham
The Holy Bible Psalm 19:1
William Shakespeare: *Hamlet* Act I, scene ii
The Holy Qur'an 006:0097 (Yusf ali Translation)
The Holy Bible: Matthew 2:1–2
The Holy Bible: Matthew 2:7
Mother Teresa
Sarah Williams (1837–1868)
inspired by an Eskimo legend
Harriet Tubman
Henry Wadsworth Longfellow, *Evangeline*

Poster by Dan Vogt

Miracles

Title	Composer/Lyricist
Angels We Have Heard on High	Traditional French carol
O Holy Night	Adolph Adam
out of print	arr. Howard Barlow
alternate arrangement	arr. Ken Berg; Marie Stultz
We Need a Little Christmas	Jerry Herman arr. Roger Emerson
Once Upon a December *Anastasia*	Stephen Flaherty & Lynn Ahrens arr. Carl Strommen
When You Believe *The Prince of Egypt*	Stephen Schwartz arr. Audrey Snyder
Angels' Carol	John Rutter
Baby, It's Cold Outside	Frank Loesser arr. Kirby Shaw
I'll Be Home for Christmas	Walter Kent/Kim Gannon arr. Mark Hayes
Ani Ma'Amin (I Believe)	Traditional Jewish text arr. John Leavitt
This Little Babe *A Ceremony of Carols*	Benjamin Britten/Robert Southwell arr. Julius Harrison
A Winter Walk	Vicki Tucker Courtney/ Herb Frombach
La Nana	Traditional Spanish carol arr. Evy Lucio
Carol of the Bells	Mykola Leontovich/ Peter J. Wilhousky arr. Peter J. Wilhousky
Ave Maria	David Childs
Litany for St. Cecilia	Jonathan Miller

If possible, use a harp for the accompaniment of "This Little Babe." Specific instrumental parts included in the music are always worth performing. Add or subtract a bit of costume when you can. Black is a great base and a colorful scarf can change the mood completely. We used winter scarves, gloves, and hats in "Baby, It's Cold Outside" and changed to all white stolas (long flowing piece of fabric worn with the ends hanging in front) for the premiere of the "Litany for St. Cecilia." This piece, written for the patron saint of music, created a spiritual effect for the singers and the audience. "Litany for St. Cecilia" is the recommended closing piece for this program. We added our traditional encore ("Silent Night" and "Night of Silence," described on page 100).

Handchimes play use the harmonized version of "Angels We Have Heard on High" from a traditional hymnal.

A link to a YouTube video of "Litany for St. Cecilia" is available at www.giamusic.com/ccc.

Miracles

> *You may use one continuous narrator or several narrators for this program. Note: The sources of the quotes used in this program are not to be read aloud by the narrator, but instead included in the program in a list at the end.*
>
> *Pre house opening: Curtain warmers up, follow spot tested and preset for first spot cue, harp preset, and stands for chimes placed in the pit.*

Opening

HANDCHIMES: Angels We Have Heard on High

> *At conclusion of prelude, students exit in a formal way. Pit lights fade and curtain warmers up. As main curtain opens, bring up stage lights.*

SECTION 1

Option 1

In the midst of all the commercialization and hurry of the Christmas season, it is all too easy to lose sight of the fact that Christmas is not about how much we can eat or how many presents we receive. Christmas is really about the birth of the Son of God. It is the miracle of that birth that should be at the heart and soul of our celebrations, and nothing else.

Option 2

What is Christmas? What do we need? *(pause)* The veil of snowflakes floating through the crisp air, the sparkle of colored lights in every window, or delicious odors drifting from the kitchen? Do we need to feel the warm cozy crackling of a glowing fireplace? Yes! And we need the sound of carols in the air.

We Need a Little Christmas

SECTION 2

Memories, whether good or bad, are a miracle in themselves, a miracle we tend to take for granted until we suddenly realize that without our memories we cannot know who we are or where we are going. Without memories we are largely helpless, for it is our past that dictates our present and it is upon our past that we build our futures. Our next song, "Once Upon a December," is from the movie *Anastasia*, and is sung by a young woman who is desperately searching for love and identity—a young woman who has lost the miracle of memory.

Once Upon a December

SECTION 3

Option 1

For a miracle to take place, we must have faith, we must believe. Even though Pharaoh is mighty and his armies vast, he is no match for the God of the Israelites. Thus the waters of the Red Sea part and—rather than being recaptured by the Egyptians and returned to servitude—Moses and his people escape to freedom. Jubilant and awed, they sing prayers of praise and thanksgiving to their Lord God.

"I will sing to the Lord, for He has triumphed gloriously,

Who is like you, oh Lord, among the celestial.

Who is like you, Majestic in holiness.

In Your love, You lead the people You redeemed.

I will sing."

Option 2

"Ah, music" he said, wiping his eyes. " A magic beyond all we do here!" (J.K. Rowling, *Harry Potter and the Sorcerer's Stone*)

When You Believe

SECTION 4

Option 1

Imagine the fear and exaltation experienced by the shepherds that cold winter night when they heard the angels singing of the miracle of Christ's birth! Having heard those glorious angel voices, the lives of those shepherds were forever changed, for who could remain untouched by such an unbelievable occurrence?

Option 2

What announces the season better than merry carolers strolling through shifting flakes of snow? At the faintest sound the doorways glow and excited children pop out to welcome visitors. It is a magical moment—one they will remember year after year!

transition: Spot out on speaker and up on stage.

Angels Carol

SECTION 5

"Baby, It's Cold Outside" was originally written to be sung by alternating voices dubbed "wolf" and "mouse" in the score. The "wolf" part is to be sung by the male and the "mouse" part is to be sung by the female. The song does not refer to any particular holiday, but due to its depiction of a snowy background, it has joined our Christmas repertoire. "Baby, It's Cold Outside" has been recorded by such greats as Dinah Shore and Buddy Clark, Ella Fitzgerald and Louis Jordan, and Louis Armstrong and Velma Middleton.

Baby, It's Cold Outside

Section 6

"I'll Be Home for Christmas" originated during World War I when it was first thought that the war would be brought to a quick conclusion and the soldiers would be returning home by Christmas time. This, of course, did not happen, hence the final line, "if only in my dreams." Twenty-five years later, during the horrors of World War II, the song touched a tender place in the hearts of Americans, both soldiers and civilians, and became the most requested song of all time at the USO Christmas shows.

I'll Be Home for Christmas

Section 7

> *Choir should enter walking slowly with a candle or votive.*

The following two songs, "Ani Ma'Amin" and "This Little Babe," are meant to be heard without interruption. We therefore respectfully request that you hold your applause until the end of the second song. Thank you.

Ani Ma'Amin

Section 8

> *As song begins, those entering from the audience walk slowly down the two aisles and onto the stage. All should be onstage and in place prior to the final amen. At the final "amen," choir members simultaneously blow out their candles. When candles are blown out, lights must blackout at same time. Still holding the bowls chest high, choir remains frozen in position. Lights slowly return to half and those singers with bowls turn and make their exit. Go immediately into "This Little Babe."*

This Little Babe

SECTION 9

The following selection, "A Winter Walk," is our Christmas card to you—our friends and families. As your card opens, you will discover inside the miracle of beauty being brought alive through the imagery of sight and sound.

A Winter Walk

SECTION 10

Originating in Spain and sung throughout Latin America, "La Nana" is a lullaby in which Mary, cooing softly to her child, asks her baby to go to sleep. Her heart is singing to her darling flower of a child, and all of her love rings through her music. There is nothing to fear, Mary assures her child, for even though night is falling, fountains are playing songs and the mockingbirds are calling.

La Nana

SECTION 11

Option 1

Not only does Mary sing to her babe, so do the bells. Joyfully ringing out in celebration, the bells send their jubilant sound both far and near. Good news! Let the heavens ring! Born is the King!

Option 2

Bells ringing and voices singing with good cheer, young and old feel merry as they hear the carolers' songs filling the air. Listen to the sweet silver bells. Throw away your cares and let every home be filled with joy.

Carol of the Bells

Section 12

Hail Mary, full of grace

The Lord is with thee.

Blessed art thou among women

And blessed is the fruit of thy womb.

Holy Mary, Mother of God,

Pray for us sinners, now and at the hour of our death.

Amen.

Ave Maria

Section 13

> *Stage crew enters with black binders, which they distribute to choir. Stolas are folded inside each binder.*

Saint Cecilia is the acclaimed patroness of music, especially church music, as well as that of musicians, composers, instrument makers, and poets. Cecilia was born to a wealthy family in the second or third century in Rome. Always sensitive to the needs of others less fortunate than herself, Cecilia ended up giving all her worldly goods to the poor. At her martyrdom, Cecilia celebrated her love of God by singing praises to him. "Litany for St. Cecilia" was composed by Jonathan Miller in 2011, almost two thousand years after her birth.

Closing

Litany of St. Cecilia

Poster by Dan Vogt

'Tis the Season

Title	Composer/Lyricist
Ríu, Ríu, Chíu	16th century Spanish carol arr. Andrey Snyder
Rise Up, Shepherd	Traditional Christmas spiritual arr. Sally Albrecht
Away in a Manger	James Spilman/anon. arr. Sherry Porterfield
Jingle Bell Rock *out of print*	Jim Beal & Jim Boothe arr. Roger Emerson
alternate arrangement	arr. Alan Billingsley
Mary, Did You Know?	Mark Lowry & Buddy Greene arr. Mac Huff
Jing-a-Ling, Jing-a-Ling	Paul Smith/Don Raye arr. Mac Huff
Gesu Bambino	Pietro Yon/Frederick Martens arr. Mac Huff
Carol of the Bells	Mykola Leontovich/ Peter J. Wilhousky arr. Peter J. Wilhousky
In the Bleak Midwinter	Gustav Holst/Christina Rossetti arr. Charles Galetar
Santa Baby	Joan Javits, Philip Springer & Tony Springer arr. Mac Huff
Go Where I Send Thee	Gospel spiritual arr. Paul Caldwell/Sean Ivory
Somebody Build a Manger	Joel Raney
Silent Night	Franz Grüber/Joseph Mohr
Night of Silence	Daniel Kantor

Add percussion instruments or a solo instrument for an individual piece when indicated. If it's December, there has to be a time to use some bells somewhere. It makes it joyful! Include them with "Jingle Bell Rock."

Adding sign language is like including another language to your program. Daniel Kantor's carol "Night of Silence," sung and signed, has become our annual tradition. It can be sung simultaneously with "Silent Night," with the accompaniment from "Night of Silence." Consider the possibility of making some type of tradition at the end of your program. Perhaps you want to invite previous choir members to join you on the stage or consider ending with the same piece of music. It could be done at any one of the programs of the year, most successfully when graduates are likely to be in town for a holiday.

A link to a YouTube video of a program excerpt is available at www.giamusic.com/ccc.

'Tis the Season

> *This program is written for two narrators. The curtain should open with the narrators and the choir in place for the first number. If possible, the choir should be humming the song "Ríu, Ríu, Chíu." The narrators will do their opening with the choir humming behind them, and should begin speaking as soon as the main act curtain is completely open. After the narrator's last line of the opening, the lights shift to the choir.*

Opening

A: The following is a series of Christmas memories as recollected by a group of students.

B: While discussing their Christmas memories and family traditions, the students decided to share their memories and traditions with you, our audience.

A: Each recollection you hear tonight represents a real person, a real family, and, as you will soon see. . .

B: the true meaning of Christmas.

A: Now please join us in celebrating, for. . .

B: 'Tis the Season!

> *Choir begins humming "Ríu, Ríu, Chíu." Narrators deliver the lines from Section 1 over the humming.*

Section 1

A: It's Christmas!

B: The holidays are here!

A: It's the time of festivities, gift giving, decorated trees, caroling, lights. . .

B: and love.

A: It's the time for families like yours and mine to come together and celebrate the birth of the Christ Child.

B: Within our family celebrations, traditions have been established, dreams fulfilled, and lasting memories made.

A: And all because, on this day, so many years ago, a child was born whose

B: name was. . .

A & B: Jesus

A: Welcome, friends, to this evening's celebration, for this is the season of Christmas!

Ríu, Ríu, Chíu

SECTION 2

B: Our first Christmas memory is centered on the celebration of a large, extended family.

A: Christmas Eve is always spent at my grandfather's house. Besides the seven members of our immediate family, there are seventeen aunts and uncles and their various husbands and wives. . .

B: and 27 cousins!

A: And according to Aunt Sarah, another little cousin is due this March, so soon there will be 28!

B: That's over 65 people!

A: And we haven't begun to count all the friends who join us!

B: One of our uncles is a priest, and we begin the evening with him saying mass. Then the older girls sing a song and the little kids act out a skit from one of the Christmas stories. After that we eat, and then it's time for the Secret Santas.

A: Each Secret Santa composes a poem, which is read aloud. Everyone else has to try to guess the recipient of that particular gift. It is always lots of fun, but what is best is having everyone in our immediate family all together for this one day out of the entire year.

Rise Up, Shepherd

SECTION 3

A: My grandma is a fanatic about the Christmas tree. The entire family works together on decorating it.

B: It has to have lots and lots of lights, and it is loaded with ornaments. Many of them are special ornaments that we use year after year.

A: I don't know why, but ever since I was a little girl, my favorite Christmas tree ornament has been one that I call "Fish Lady." "Fish Lady" is a sassy purple fish with lips painted a bright glittery red. (*Reader sighs wistfully.*) I have always wanted lipstick just that color. You may be sure that I am the one who always hangs "Fish Lady" on the tree.

B: When we have finished our decorating job, we turn off all the lights sit around our beautiful tree, and sing Christmas songs like "Away in the Manger," "Jingle Bells," and "The Twelve Days of Christmas."

A: It's lovely.

Away in a Manger

SECTION 4

B: It was on December 23, just two days before Christmas, when my parents made the adoption of my older twin sisters official. Even though I had yet to be been born, that December 23rd was when the two most important people in my life came to live in my family.

A: My sister's names are Jazmyn and Joclyn, and to this day, they are the best Christmas presents I have ever received!

Jingle Bell Rock

SECTION 5

A: Have you ever yearned for a special gift? Well, I have. There was one particular gift that I had wanted for *so* long. What I wanted was a pair of roller skates, but I didn't want just any ordinary roller skates! Oh no. The skates I wanted were special: They were pink and white, and they had little pink and white pompoms with bells in them fastened onto the toes. I wanted those skates so badly because I just knew that with those skates on my feet, I would be able to skate backwards, do fancy spins, and even dance! But no matter how much I wished for those pink and white skates, there were no skates for my birthday, no skates for any of the holidays.

B: And then, one year under the Christmas tree, there they were! My roller skates! I have never, ever been happier. I have those skates to this day, and whenever I wear them, I am in a whole different world—my own world—a world where I am always laughing and happy.

Mary, Did You Know?

SECTION 6

B: For those of us who are of Polish heritage, Christmas Eve is called *Wigilia,* and it is a most special family time. In my family Christmas Eve is made even more special because it is also my grandma's birthday. To celebrate, we have a family dinner.

A: Our Christmas Eve dinner is always a traditional Polish meal. No meat is served at this meal. Instead we have *barsez* soup, which is beet soup. Then we break *oplatki*, which is a thin wafer with scenes of the Nativity on it. Every person sitting around the table breaks off a little piece of the wafer and eats it and then we say a blessing and wish other people good health and good luck.

Jing-a-Ling, Jing-a-Ling

SECTION 7

B: We do not always spend Christmas here at home. Often my family and I go either to Poland or to Italy for Christmas.

A: I don't mind if we're not at home, because no matter where I am for Christmas, as long as I am with my family, I am fine.

B: Last Christmas we went to Italy and there we had the best Christmas ever, for I stood as Godmother for my little cousin, Stefano. I was so thrilled! The memories still make me smile.

Gesu Bambino

SECTION 8

A: Last year at Christmas time my family decided not to give gifts to each other. Instead, we all went to New York City to celebrate the holidays. My brother had been away at school in New York, and we hadn't seen him for a long time and we missed him. He missed us, too, so we decided that the gift we all wanted most was to be able to spend time together.

B: Gifts aren't as important as being together. Christmas is really about family and Jesus, and not about Santa and presents.

Carol of the Bells

SECTION 9

A: I always go to Nana's house during Advent and help her getting ready for Christmas Eve. I love being with her. We make *kolacki* cookies and nut cups, and decorate the house.

B: On the morning of Christmas Eve we do the final house cleaning, cut the bread, and make the salad for Christmas dinner. I enjoy doing all this, for it seems to slow down the season.

A: I love all aspects of the holidays, but what I love most is that Christmas is about spending time together with the people I love, not just thinking about buying things.

Option 1

B: Christmas is about family and God, and the celebration of both. It's about Jesus and the celebration of his birth.

Option 2

B: Christmas is about family and friends, and the celebration of spending time together.

In the Bleak Midwinter

Section 10

A: One Christmas Eve my family and I were visiting at my grandparent's house. All my cousins were there, too, but I was one of the youngest and at a very mischievous age. Even though I was very young, I still managed to convince one of my other cousins to join me in breaking into the Christmas closet and checking out all the gifts.

B: You did *what?!* I can't believe it!

A: (*nods head regretfully*) I hate to admit it, but it's true. We got into the closet easily enough, but to our great disappointment, all of the gifts were wrapped! The best we could do was to check them all out, read the nametags, see how big the presents were and find out who got the most!

B: Didn't you get caught?

A: No, thank heavens! And believe me, I never did it again! It isn't worth spoiling the surprise and fun of opening gifts on Christmas morning.

Santa Baby

SECTION 11

A: One Christmas my parents invited our friends from Cape Town, South Africa, to visit us for the holidays. Our friends were delighted to be joining us, if for no other reason than they had never before seen snow.

B: We took them everywhere, sharing our Christmas traditions and the sights and sounds of the holiday season, but what was most joyful was to have Christmas dinner with them.

A: We learned that in Cape Town people eat very different food from us. For example, for Christmas dinner they eat spicy African dishes, and jerk chicken with rice.

B: Our friends told us how blessed we are here in the United States, because in South Africa many, many children don't get any Christmas gifts at all.

Go Where I Send Thee

SECTION 12

A: One year on Christmas day there was a big snowstorm, so my dad and all of us kids put on our snow gear, went outside, and made a *ginormous* snowman. It was so big we had to lift the top snowballs up with a trashcan lid.

B: The snowman had a carrot nose and a corncob pipe, just like snowmen are supposed to have. We positioned him carefully between two fir trees, facing the dining room window. All around him we made lots of little snowmen and in his arms we placed a carefully lettered sign.

A: Now, Christmas is also my Grammy's birthday, and so that afternoon we sat with Grammy at the dining room table, making sure that her back was to the picture window. At just the right moment we yelled, "Okay, you can turn around now, Grammy!" and when she did, there it was, right in the middle of the window! Perfectly framed between the two fir trees was our ginormous snowman, holding a big sign that read, "Happy Birthday, Grammy!"

Somebody Build a Manger

SECTION 13

A: Christmas memories are precious, for when we look back we realize how significant they are, how they impact our lives, and how they make us who we are today.

B: On Christmas Eve we light a fire, drink hot chocolate, and sing Christmas songs. On Christmas Day we have more music and open our gifts one at a time to make it last longer.

A: Christmas traditions passed on are a wonderful security—and they're fun, too!

B: Christmas is the time the whole family can be together. Everybody comes to celebrate Christmas, and that is what makes it so very special!

Silent Night and Night of Silence

> *Our tradition with most Christmas programs is to end with "Silent Night" and "Night of Silence." Sing "Silent Night" and "Night of Silence" separately, and then simultaneously with the accompaniment from "Night of Silence." They could also be performed as an encore.*

Optional Ending

AUDIENCE joins in singing Deck the Hall

Choral Repertoire Inventory

Key: Publishers

Boosey	Boosey & Hawkes
ECS	EC Schirmer
Fischer	Carl Fischer
HL	Hal Leonard
OUP	Oxford University Press
UE	Universal Edition

Program titles

Angels	Angels	Light	A Light in the Night
Beatles	Back to the Beatles	Miracles	Miracles
Birds	The Birds and the Bees	Moments	Moments from Musicals
Colors	Colors of Christmas	Musical	Musical Conversations
Food	Food, Fun, and Festivities!	Nature	And Nature Sings
Joyful	Be Joyful!	Season	'Tis the Season
		Spirit	The Spirit Says Sing!

Title	Composer	Lyrics	Arranger	Publisher	Voicings	Program
A Nightingale Sang in Berkeley Square	Sherwin	Maschwitz	Billingsley	HL	SATB•SSA	Birds
A Winter Walk	Courtney	Frombach		BriLee	SSA	Miracles
Ain'-a That Good News	Spiritual		Dawson	Kjos	SSAA•SATB	Spirit
Ain't Misbehavin'	Waller & Brooks	Razaf	Shackley	Alfred	SATB•SAB•SSA	Moments
All You Need is Love	Lennon & McCartney	Lennon & McCartney	Billingsley	HL	SATB•SAB•2-part	Beatles
Alleluia! I Will Sing	Waggoner			Alfred	2-part	Joyful
And All That Jazz	Kander	Ebb	Shaw	Alfred	SATB•SAB•SSA	Moments
Angels' Carol	Rutter	Rutter		Hinshaw	SATB•2-part	Miracles
Angels, Spread Your Loving Wings	Schram	Busch		BriLee	SSA	Angels
Angels Watchin' over Me	Spiritual		Simms	BriLee	SSA	Light
Angels We Have Heard on High	French carol	Chadwick	Huff	HL	SSA	Miracles•Angels
Ani Ma'amin (I Believe)	Trad. Jewish		Leavitt	HL	SATB•SAB•SSAB•TTB	Miracles
At the River	Hymn adapt. Copland		Wilding-White	Boosey	SSA•SATB•SA•Unison	Nature

147

COMPELLING CHORAL CONCERTS — LINDA CRABTREE POWELL

Title	Composer	Lyrics	Arranger	Publisher	Voicings	Program
Ave Maria	Childs			SBMP	SSA	Miracles
Ave Maria	Kodály			UE	SSA	Angels
Ave Maria (Angelus Domini)	Biebl	Liturgical chant		Hinshaw	SSAATTBB•SATB•SSAA•TTBB	Colors
Away in a Manger	Spilman	Anon.	Porterfield	Alfred	SSA	Season
Baby, It's Cold Outside	Loesser		Shaw	HL	SATB•SAB•SSA	Miracles•Food
Barter	Clausen	Teasdale		SBMP	SSA	Musical
Beacon Hill Carol	Irish air		Hatfield	Boosey	3-part treble	Colors
Believe	Silvestri & Ballard	Silvestri & Ballard	Hayes	Alfred	SATB•SSAB•SSA•2-part	Joyful
Blackbird	Lennon & McCartney	Lennon & McCartney	Brymer	HL	SATB•SAB	Birds
Blue Christmas	Hayes & Johnson	Hayes & Johnson	Huff	HL	SATB•TTBB•SAB	Colors
Blue Moon	Rogers	Hart	Althouse	Alfred	SATB•SAB•SSA	Birds
Blue Skies	Berlin	Berlin	Emerson	HL	SATB•3-part mixed•2-part	Birds
Breakaway	Gerrard, Lavigne & Benenate	Gerrard, Lavigne & Benenate	Chinn	Alfred	SATB•3-part mixed	Birds
Breath of Heaven	Grant & Eaton	Grant & Eaton	Emerson	HL	SATB•SAB•SSA•2-part	Joyful
Bridge over Troubled Water	Simon	Simon	Shaw	Shawnee	SATB•SAB•SSA•TTBB	Nature
Bumble Bee	Edenroth	Edenroth		Walton	SSAATB•SSAA	Birds
Carol of the Bells	Leontovich	Wilhousky	Wilhousky	Fischer	SATB•SAB•SSA•TTBB	Angels•Joyful•Colors•Light•Season•Miracles
Castle on a Cloud	Schonberg	Kretzmer	Spevacek	HL	SSA•SATB•2-part	Moments

CHORAL REPERTOIRE INVENTORY

Title	Composer	Lyrics	Arranger	Publisher	Voicings	Program
Child of God	Spiritual		Crocker	HL	SATB•2-part	Colors
Christmas Time Is Here	Mendelson & Guaraldi	Mendelson & Guaraldi	Chinn	Warner	2-part	Colors
Colors of Winter	Bernon	Bernon		Heritage	SAB•SSA•2-part	Colors
Cool Yule	Allen	Allen	Shaw	HL	SATB•SAB•SSA•2-part	Colors
Count Your Blessings Instead of Sheep	Berlin	Berlin	Miller	HL	2-part	Joyful
Crawdad Hole	American folk song		Goetze	Boosey	SSA	Spirit
Crossing the Bar	Walker	Tennyson		ECS	SATB•SSAA•TTBB	Musical
Dance of the Sugar Plum Fairy	Tchaikovsky		Funk	Alfred	SATB•3-part mixed•SSAA	Light•Food
Dona Nobis Pacem	Anon. 16th c.		Hopson	Hope	SAB•2-part	Nature
Down to the River to Pray	Traditional		Curry	HL	SATB•SAB•2-part	Nature
Dust in the Wind	Livgren	Livgren	Emerson	HL	SATB•SAB•2-part	Nature
Eleanor Rigby	Lennon & McCartney	Lennon & McCartney	Emerson	HL	SATB•SAB•SSA	Beatles
Evening Prayer from *Hansel & Gretel*	Humperdinck		Snyder	HL	SSA•2-part	Angels
Feed the Birds	Sherman & Sherman	Sherman & Sherman	Miller	HL	2-part	Birds
Fly Me to the Moon	Howard	Howard	Shaw	HL	SATB•SAB•SSA	Nature
Food, Glorious Food	Bart	Bart	Lewis	HL	2-part	Food
For the Beauty of the Earth	Rutter	Pierpoint		Hinshaw	SATB•SA•TTBB	Nature
Forget About the Boy	Tesori	Scanlan	Snyder	HL	SSA	Moments
Gesu Bambino	Yon	Martens	Huff	HL	SSA	Season

149

Title	Composer	Lyrics	Arranger	Publisher	Voicings	Program
Go, Tell It on the Mountain	Spiritual		Simms	Alfred	2-part	Light
Go Where I Send Thee	Gospel spiritual		Caldwell & Ivory	earthsongs	SATB•TTB•SSA	Season
Good King Kong Looked Out	Schickele (P.D.Q. Bach)	Schickele		Presser	SATB•SAB•SSAA	Joyful
Good Night	Lennon & McCartney	Lennon & McCartney	Snyder	HL	SATB•SAB•2-part	Beatles
Hail Holy Queen	Trad.	Trad. hymn, adapt. Emerson	Shaiman	HL	SATB•SSA•2-part	Joyful
Happy Together	Bonner & Gordon		Jasperse	Shawnee	SATB	Beatles
Hello, Goodbye	Lennon & McCartney	Lennon & McCartney	Billingsley	HL	SATB•SAB•SSA	Beatles
Here Comes the Sun	Harrison	Harrison	Billingsley	HL	SATB•SAB•SSA	Beatles
Hey Jude	Lennon & McCartney	Lennon & McCartney	Sharon	HL	SSA	Beatles
Hole in the Bucket	American folk song		Sheppard & Jones	Boston	SATB	Spirit
The Holly and the Ivy	Old English carol		Jeffers	earthsongs	SSA	Joyful
The Holly and the Ivy	Old English carol		Stone	Pro Art	SSA	Joyful
Home	Smalls	Smalls	Beck & Spresser	Warner	SATB•SSAB•2-part	Moments
Hot Chocolate	Ballard & Silvestri	Ballard & Silvestri	Emerson	HL	SATB•3-part mixed•2-part	Joyful•Food
How Can I Keep from Singing?	Lowry		Beck	Alfred	SATB•SAB•SSA	Spirit
Hush! Somebody's Callin' My Name	Trad. spiritual		Dennard	Shawnee	2-part	Spirit
I Dream a World	Dilworth	Hughes		HL	SATB•SSA	Musical

CHORAL REPERTOIRE INVENTORY

Title	Composer	Lyrics	Arranger	Publisher	Voicings	Program
I'll Be Home for Christmas	Kent	Gannon	Hayes	Alfred	SATB•SAB•SSA•TTBB	Miracles
I'll Give My Love an Apple	English folk song		Daley	Alliance	SSA	Food
I'm Gonna Sing When the Spirit Says Sing	Traditional spiritual		Helvey	Beckenhorst	SATB•TTBB	Spirit
If I Can Stop One Heart from Breaking	Meier	Dickinson	Kupferschmid	HL	SSA	Musical
If I Fell in Love with You	Lennon & McCartney	Lennon & McCartney		Warner	Unison	Beatles
If Music Be the Food of Love	Beck	Shakespeare & Beck		Alfred	SATB•SSAB	Musical
Il est né, le divin enfant	Fauré	French carol; Sisson	Sisson	ABI	Unison or 2-part	Angels
Imagine	Lennon & McCartney	Lennon & McCartney	Huff	HL	SATB•SAB•SSA	Beatles
In the Bleak Midwinter	Holst	Rossetti	Galetar	National	SSA	Season
It's the Most Wonderful Time of the Year	Pola & Wyle	Pola & Wyle	Billingsley	Alfred	SATB•3-part mixed•2-part	Joyful
Jesu, Joy of Man's Desiring	Bach		Riegger	Shawnee	SATB•SAB•SSA•TTBB•2-part mixed	Light
Jing-a-Ling, Jing-a-Ling	Smith	Raye	Huff	HL	SATB•SSA•SAB	Season
Jingle Bell Rock	Beal & Boothe	Beal & Boothe	Billingsley	Alfred	SATB•SAB•SSA•2-part	Season
Jingle Bell Rock	Beal & Boothe	Beal & Boothe	Emerson	HL	SSA	Season
Jingle Bells	Pierpont	Pierpont, adapt. Hayes	Gold & Paich	Alfred	SATB•SSA•TTBB	Food
Jingle Bells Hallelujah	Pierpoint & Handel		Miller	SESM	SATB	Colors
Jonah	Dilworth	Dilworth		HL	SATB•SSA•TTB	Musical
Jordan's Angels	Dilworth; spiritual	Dilworth		HL	SATB•SSA•2-part	Angels

151

COMPELLING CHORAL CONCERTS   LINDA CRABTREE POWELL

Title	Composer	Lyrics	Arranger	Publisher	Voicings	Program
Joyfully Sing!	Spevacek	Spevacek		HL	SSA	Joyful
Kyrie	Schubert	trans. Liebergen	Liebergen	Alfred	SAT•SAB•SSA	Angels
La Nana	Spanish carol	trans. Lucio	Lucio	Kjos	SSA	Miracles
Let It Be	Lennon & McCartney	Lennon & McCartney	Brymer	HL	SATB•SAB•SSAA	Beatles
Linus and Lucy	Guaraldi		Kern	Shawnee	SSA•SSAB•TTBB•SATB	Joyful
Litany for St. Cecilia	Miller		Miller	SESM	SSAA	Miracles
Little Horses	Appalachian folk song, adapt. Copland		Wilding-White	Boosey	SSA	Spirit
Lo, How a Rose E'er Blooming	16th c., Praetorius	Baker	Shand	ECS	SSA	Angels
Lo, How a Rose E'er Blooming	16th c., Praetorius	German melody	Leavitt	HL	SATB•TTBB	Angels
Long and Winding Road	Lennon & McCartney	Lennon & McCartney	Langford	Sony	SATB	Beatles
Mary, Did You Know?	Lowry & Greene	Lowry & Greene	Huff	HL	SSAA	Season
Memory	Lloyd Webber	Nunn, T. S. Eliot	Lojeski	HL	SATB•SAB•SSA•2-part	Moments
Merrily Sing Noel!	Spevacek	Spevacek		Heritage	SATB•SSA•TBB	Joyful
Merry Christmas Darling	Pooler & Carpenter	Pooler & Carpenter	Huff	HL	SATB•SSA	Light
A Midsummer Night's Dream	Mendelssohn	Shakespeare	Crocker	HL	3-part treble	Musical
Mister Sandman	Ballard	Ballard	Lojeski	HL	SSAA•SAB•2-part	Spirit
Monotone Angel	McAfee	McAfee		Alfred	SSA•SATB	Angels
Morning has Broken	Trad. Scottish	Farjeon	Simeone	Shawnee	SATB•SAB•SSA•2-part	Birds

152

CHORAL REPERTOIRE INVENTORY

Title	Composer	Lyrics	Arranger	Publisher	Voicings	Program
My Favorite Things	Rodgers	Hammerstein	Huff	HL	SATB•SAB•SSA•2-part	Joyful•Food
Never Never Land	Styne	Comden & Green	Huff	HL	SAATB•SSA	Moments
Night of Silence	Kantor, Grüber	Kantor	Kantor	GIA	Unison	Season•Angels•Light•Miracles
Not While I'm Around	Sondheim	Sondheim	Brymer	HL	SATB•SAB•2-part	Moments
Now is the Month of Maying	Morley		Ehret; Wilson	Boosey	SSA	Birds
O Holy Night	Adam	Cappeau; Dwight	Berg	Fischer	SATB	Miracles
O Holy Night	Adam	Cappeau; Dwight	Stultz	Morning Star	Unison•2-part	Miracles
O Holy Night	Adam	Cappeau; Dwight	Strickling	H&M	SSA	Miracles
Ob-La-Di, Ob-La-Da	Lennon & McCartney	Lennon & McCartney	Brymer	HL	3-part mixed•2-part	Beatles
Once Upon a December	Flaherty	Ahrens	Strommen	Alfred	Two-part	Miracles
Over the Rainbow	Arlen	Harburg	Robinson	Alfred	SATB•SSAA	Nature•Moments
Parsley, Sage, Rosemary, and Thyme	Old English song		Coates	Shawnee	SATB•SSA	Food•Spirit
Patapan	Burgundian carol	La Monnoye; Peter	Peter	Morning-Star	SSAA	Joyful
Penny Lane	Lennon & McCartney	Lennon & McCartney	Snyder	HL	SSAA•SA	Beatles
Poor Mary	Davis		Cowley	Fischer	SATB•SSA	Colors
Poor Wayfaring Stranger	Trad. folk spiritual		Christopher	HL	SATB•SAB•TTB	Spirit
Prayer	Humperdinck	Wette; Marlhom	Riegger	Flammer	2-part	Angels
Rise Up, Shepherd	Trad. spiritual	Albrecht	Albrecht	Alfred	SATB•SSA	Season

153

Title	Composer	Lyrics	Arranger	Publisher	Voicings	Program
Ríu, Ríu, Chíu	16th c. Spanish	trans. Black	Snyder	HL	3-part mixed•2-part	Season
Rockin' Robin	Thomas	Thomas	Emerson	HL	3-part mixed•2-part	Birds
Route 66	Troup		Emerson	HL	SSA•3-part mixed•2-part	Musical
'S Wonderful	Gershwin	Gershwin	Robinson	Alfred	SATB•SAB	Moments
'S Wonderful	Gershwin	Gershwin	Warnick	New World	SSA	Moments
Santa Baby	Javits, Springer, Springer		Huff	HL	SSA	Season
Shenandoah	American folk song		Erb	Alfred	SSAATTBB•TTBB•SSAA	Nature
Shine	John	Hall	Brymer	HL	SSA	Moments
Silent Night	Grüber	Mohr		GIA	unison	Season•Angels•Miracles•Light
Silver Bells	Livingston & Evans	Livingston & Evans	Terry	Hansen	TTBB•SSA	Colors
Simple Gifts	Shaker tune		Althouse	Alfred	SATB•SSAB•SSAA	Spirit
Simple Gifts	Shaker tune		Wheeler	BriLee	SSA	Spirit
Simple Gifts	Shaker tune		Kirk	Belwin	SSA	Spirit
Sing a Joyful Song	Simms	Simms		HL	3-part mixed•2-part	Joyful
Sing for Joy!	Handel	Spevacek	Spevacek		2-part	Joyful
Singin' in the Rain	Brown	Freed	Schram	Alfred	SATB•2-part	Moments
Sleigh Ride	Anderson	Parish	Beck	Alfred	SATB•SAB•2-part	Light•Food
Somebody Build a Manger	Raney	Raney		Hope	SATB	Season

CHORAL REPERTOIRE INVENTORY

Title	Composer	Lyrics	Arranger	Publisher	Voicings	Program
Stormy Weather	Arlen	Koehler	Lojeski	HL	SSA	Nature
Summertime	Gershwin	Heyward, Gershwin	Hayes	Alfred	SATB•SSAB•SSA•TTBB	Moments•Musical
The Birds and the Bees	Newman	Newman		Spirit One	Unison	Birds
The Christmas Song	Tormé & Wells	Tormé & Wells	Shaw	HL	SATB•SSAA	Colors•Angels
The Raven Watches Me	Courtney	Parker (Poe)		Shawnee	3-part mixed	Musical
The River Sleeps beneath the Sky	Lightfoot	Dunbar		Heritage	SATB•3-part mixed•SSA	Musical
The Snow	Elgar	Elgar		Novello	SATB•SSA	Food
The Tell-Tale Heart	Lewis & Habash	Lewis & Habash (Poe)	Habash	Orpheus	SAB	Musical
The Wind	Schram	Schram		Alfred	2-part	Nature
This Little Babe	Britten	Southwell	Harrison	Boosey	SATB•SSA	Miracles
Till There Was You	Willson	Willson	Huff	HL	SATB•SSA	Birds
Tonight	Bernstein	Sondheim	Stickles	Alfred	SATB•SAB•SSA	Moments
Try to Remember	Schmidt	Jones	Althouse	Alfred	SATB•SAB•2-part•SSA	Moments
The Turtle Dove	Folk song		Purifoy	HL	SAB•SATB	Birds
Two Wassails	Trad. English carols		Johnson	OUP	SSA	Light
Ubi Caritas	Gjeilo	Gjeilo		Walton	SATB•SSAA•TTBB	Light
Velvet Shoes	Thompson	Wylie	Seitz	ECS	SSAATTBB•2-part	Food
Wassail!	Trad. English carol		Rubino	HL	SATB	Light

Title	Composer	Lyrics	Arranger	Publisher	Voicings	Program
We Need a Little Christmas	Herman	Herman	Emerson	HL	3-Part mixed•2-part	Miracles
We Three Kings	Hopkins	Hopkins	Robinson	Fischer	SATB•TBB	Joyful
What Child Is This	Anon. English	Dix		GIA	unison	Colors•Light
What Strangers Are These?	Old Scottish carol	Old Scottish carol	Forrest	Beckenhorst	SATB•SSA	Joyful
When I'm Sixty-Four	Lennon & McCartney	Lennon & McCartney	Billingsley	HL	SATB•SAB•SSA	Beatles
When the Red, Red Robin	Woods	Woods	Simeone	Shawnee	SSA	Birds
When You Believe	Schwartz	Schwartz	Snyder	HL	SATB•SAB•2-part	Miracles
White Christmas	Berlin	Berlin	Ringwald	HL	SATB•SSA•TTB	Colors•Light
Windy Nights	Gray	Stevenson		Heritage	3-part mixed•2-part	Musical
Winter Carnival	Danish folk dance	Whitmore	Spevacek	Heritage	SATB•3-part mixed	Food
Winter Wonderland	Bernard	Smith	Arnaud	Shawnee	SATB	Colors
Won't You Join the Dance?	Ginsberg	Carroll		Heritage	SSA	Musical
Wouldn't It Be Loverly?	Loewe	Lerner	Noelte	Chappell	SSA	Moments
Yesterday	Lennon & McCartney	Lennon & McCartney	Brymer	HL	SATB•SAB•SSA	Beatles
You Can't Stop the Beat	Shaiman	Shaiman & Wittman	Emerson	HL	SATB•SAB•SSA•2-part	Moments

About the Authors

An experienced and noted choral teacher, Linda Crabtree Powell has perfected the art of choral programming. With musical selections that both challenge and educate her students, these themes are eagerly anticipated each season. Her choirs have traveled and performed extensively including Canada, Ireland, and Spain. She has taught all levels of music, worked as a clinician and accompanist, and founded B.R.A.V.O.! program in Oak Park, Illinois. She currently sings with the Michael Teolis Singers.

Ms. Powell graduated from the University of Michigan with a Bachelor of Music with Distinction and a Masters of Music in Piano from the American Conservatory of Music. She lives in River Forest, Illinois and spends as much time as possible in Italy. As written on her kindergarten report card, "likes to sing and make up songs." Now, Linda is also making up choral programs for others to use and enjoy.

Valerie Sokol (1942–2013) received her BA in Theater and English Literature from Lake Forest College and her master's degree in Theater from Northern Illinois University. She performed, directed, and wrote for the stage for over thirty-five years. Her experience encompassed plays, children's theater, musicals, reviews, and one-woman shows. For twenty-five years at Downers Grove North High School in Illinois, Mrs. Sokol taught acting classes, creative writing, and English. "Writing for choirs is a true joy for me," Sokol said, "for they always combine three of my favorite things: beautiful music, fun writing, and the finer elements of stage performance."

Julia Buckley received a BA in English from Valparaiso University and a master's degree in Language Studies from Elmhurst College. She is a high school teacher and a published writer of mystery novels, including *The Dark Backward* (2006) and *The Ghosts of Lovely Women* (2010). She will soon complete the first novel in a series for Berkley Prime Crime. She enjoys working with young people and teaching literature, and she was pleased to be able to collaborate with her colleague and friend, Linda Crabtree Powell.